Word 2000

Linda Steven

An imprint of PEARSON EDUCATION

PEARSON EDUCATION LIMITED

Head Office:
Edinburgh Gate
Harlow
Essex CM20 2JE
Tel: +44 (0) 1279 623623
Fax: +44 (0) 1279 431059

London Office:
128 Long Acre
London WC2E 9AN
Tel: +44 (0) 171 447 2000
Fax: +44 (0) 171 240 5771

First published in Great Britain 2000

© Pearson Education Limited 2000

First published in 1999 as
Se Former En Un Jour: Word 2000
by CampusPress France
19, rue Michel Le Comte
75003 Paris
France

Library of Congress Cataloging in Publication Data
Available from the publisher.

British Library Cataloguing in Publication Data
A CIP catalogue record for this book can be obtained from the British Library.

ISBN 0-13-026259-5

10   9   8   7   6   5   4   3   2   1

Translated and typeset by Cybertechnics, Sheffield.
Printed and bound in Great Britain by Ashford Colour Press, Gosport, Hampshire.

The publishers' policy is to use paper manufactured from sustainable forests.

Contents

Contents

Introduction

....

■ Word 2000: communication and simplification

The main improvements added to this version of the most widely used of Windows word processor make Word 2000 even more user-friendly and Internet-compatible. The principles of page layout have been simplified and improved; the treatment of graphics, for example, is now of professional quality. A few summary actions will transform a Word 2000 document into a Web page or into e-mail, ready to be sent at a click of the mouse.

■ Simplified page layout

Word 2000 contains many new ideas for automatic formatting. Already in the previous version, headings and bulleted (or numbered) lists could be automatically applied. For each type of document (letter, e-mail and so on) there was a specific template. Now typing and formatting text can be done simultaneously. This function is useful for creating headings, headers or tables; even tables within tables. The embellishment of text using shortcut keys is also possible.

■ Grammatical corrections as you type

Correcting spelling and grammar while typing in Word 2000 is more efficient than in Word 97. The majority of typing and spelling mistakes and the more common grammatical errors are corrected automatically. Amongst other things, this function allows the automatic insertion of both text and graphics or symbols. It can be optionally deactivated.

■ Numerous graphic effects

Word 97 (or Word 8) already surpassed Word 7 with WordArt 3-D effects. Documents became much better presented. Thanks to new functions in Word 2000, it is now possible to create presentations of professional quality. At last you will be able to compete with computer graphics artists.

Word 2000 offers more than 150 new basic borders, with numerous variation possibilities. Page borders are supplemented by text borders which allow page headers or certain paragraphs to be brought to the fore. One hundred and sixty coloured styles have been added, simultaneously taking account of the more general use of both colour printers and high-resolution screens. To profit best from this, you should choose the 24-bit colour setting for your computer display. Your shadow effects will then have colour gradations.

WordArt has become Office Art. Objects incorporated in documents are now independent and you can define levels of layering and zones of transparency.

Blocks of text can be independent or connected, which allows text to flow from one block to another. List hierarchy elements are treated as objects; they can therefore be replaced by pictures. Word 2000 offers, at this level, all the convenience of Web pages that handle objects in HTML.

■ A 12-item Clipboard

The Clipboard can now hold up to 12 selections. The **Cut**, **Copy** and **Paste** functions have become more user-friendly. Now you can store pictures or text for use elsewhere without having to delete already stored items.

■ Automated summary and resumé

Already available in Word 97, the **AutoSummarize** function allows showing, on the right of the screen, the outline of a document and, on the left, its key phrases or groups of significant words. Word 2000 offers, in addition, an automatic resumé of unlimited size, which can be presented separately.

■ Easily created tables

Inserting a table is now a simple operation, fast and very effective. Users who were deterred by tables will manipulate this new version with a smile on their lips. You can specify the number and location of columns, and make all kinds of modifications.

Managing the cells which make up a table has also become more flexible. Stylised text can be integrated in them and rotated in steps of 90°. This allows certain conventions to be met, such as that copyright be mentioned at the side of rather than below an illustration. Now cells are treated as objects which, by their nature, can contain other objects.

■ Creating Styles

Style sheets are very useful. They allow the standardisation of documents with the same structure. You can now create them from the current document, making it a document template. The expanding **Styles** list, from the Formatting toolbar, offers a preview, which avoids any need to open a dialog box.

■ Communication via the Internet

The most spectacular improvement of this version is the interlink between text processing and the Internet. To access the Internet, you only need to manipulate the Internet toolbar. Word 2000 is always in a position to create HTML pages and to generate hypertext links but, using Outlook, it allows e-mail to be sent directly. Obviously, those who benefit most will be dedicated Microsoft users, since they will be able to retrieve pictures as well as various improvements. By this link, the presentation of your mail can be considerably improved.

Uniform Resource Locator (URL) addresses designating the address of Web sites were already automatically activated in Word 97. A double-click is all that is needed to access them. For those who work on an intranet, Word 2000 allows online meetings as well as document sharing. These improvements are an aid to group working and the pooling of ideas.

The integration of HTML allows you to save any existing document as a Web page to your hard disk, Internet, or Web server, complete with frames. The Word interface includes such current Web features as dialog boxes and scrolled lists.

The Word environment changes from that of a word processor into a space for simple programming and sophisticated publishing. A Word 2000 HTML document can be edited directly on a remote server, hence on the Web. You can even append scripts to it!

■ Click and type technique

Previously, a new document opened as a blank white page; you could not click just anywhere on it. Now, in Word 2000, you can easily insert text or a picture at any location on the page. To use this technique you must be working in **Page Layout** mode.

■ Some new assistants

Finally, Word 2000 offers some new **Office Assistants**. The Create Mail assistant, for example, integrates a history with document distribution. It allows your mail sendings and senders' replies to be saved. An expanded list gives access to the termination fields, allowing the insertion of a predefined letter ending.

The Office Assistants are covered in detail in the next chapters.

■ Symbols

Under this heading, you will find additional information.

This symbol warns you about problems you may encounter in certain cases. It also warns you what not to do. If you follow these instructions, you should not have any problems.

 This symbol provides you with suggestions and tips: keyboard shortcuts, advanced techniques, and so on.

1

Discovering the software

Text processing is a valuable tool for both planning and completing written work, and can help you equally with the templates and forms. Word 2000 is one of the most productive software programs on the market. It is useful for both professionals and occasional users. It is so simple to use that even people with no previous experience of word-processing packages will find it user-friendly.

■ Installing Word 2000

Required configuration

To install Word 2000, you need a computer set-up comprising:

- a Pentium or a DX 400;
- Windows 95 or 98;
- at least 16 megabytes of RAM (Random Access Memory, or main memory)
- a hard disk;
- a CD-ROM drive;
- a Windows compatible screen;
- a Microsoft compatible mouse.

 *In contrast to **ROM**, which is read-only memory, **RAM** is available for both reading and writing.*

Installing Word 2000

To install Word 2000, perform the following steps:

1. Switch on your computer and start **Windows**.
2. Insert the **Word 2000** disk into your CD-ROM drive.
3. Select the **Installation** button.
4. Follow the instructions which appear in sequence in the program installation dialog boxes (for further details, see Appendix A).

■ Starting Word 2000

After switching on, the first task is to start Word 2000: click on the **Start** icon on the taskbar at the bottom of the screen.

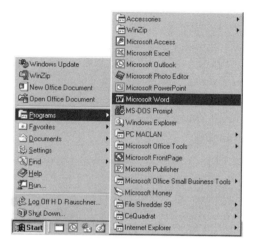

Figure 1.1 Click on the Start icon on the taskbar and select the Programs option.

Selecting the **Programs** option displays a submenu in which Word 2000 is listed under the name of Microsoft Word.

*If you use Word frequently, add a shortcut to your desktop to bypass the **Start** menu. To create a shortcut on the desktop, right-click on the **Microsoft Word** entry in the **Programs** submenu and drag-and-drop it on the desktop. In the context menu that opens on the desktop, select **Create Shortcut(s) Here**.*

Once the word processor has started, a blank document will appear. The cursor, displayed as a vertical blinking bar, marks the starting point of your text. But before starting to type, you should configure Word 2000 to personalise it for your own use.

■ Configuring Word 2000

Configuring your word processor consists in adapting it to your requirements and habits – which might, for example, concern the choice of a font size.

Fonts

The expression 'font' means a set of characters with the same typeface. We shall select the Book Antiqua **font**:

1. Open the **Format** menu.

2. Select the **Font** option.

3. In the **Font** tab, scroll down the list of fonts.

4. Click on **Book Antiqua**.

Now select a size of 10 for this font. You can proceed in one of two ways:

■ Use the **Font Size** box next to the **Font** box on the **Formatting** toolbar. Click the arrow to the right of the **Font Size** box to scroll down the list and select a font size.

■ In the **Format** menu, select **Font**. Word 2000 offers about 100 fonts whose size and style you can modify. You can also add other fonts available on the market.

More about fonts in Chapter 3.

 *Word 2000 automatically installs fonts in a Windows directory called Fonts. The access path to this folder is C:\Windows\Fonts. These are, for the most part, **TrueType** fonts. These are signalled by the abbreviation TT. These fonts offer a large range of sizes and styles.*

■ On the **Character Spacing** tab, you will find options for spacing letters within a word, setting their distance from the baseline, and their scale.

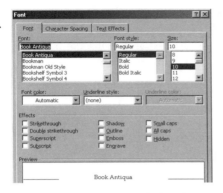

**Figure 1.2 Selecting the Book Antiqua font
in the Font tab of the Font dialog box.**

■ On the **Text Effects** tab, you will find the **Animations** list
with a set of options for animating letters with surround
effects.

The **Las Vegas Lights** animation effect, for example, surrounds
each word with stars and flashing dots.

**Figure 1.3 Selecting the Las Vegas Lights animation
in the Text Effects tab of the Font dialog box.**

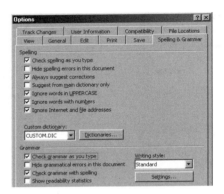

Figure 1.4 The Check grammar as you type option.

If you want to make other settings before typing your first document, open the **Tools** menu and select the **Options** command which offers a large choice of settings (spelling, grammar, printing, viewing and editing). You can, for example, arrange for your spelling and grammar to be checked as you type. But careful, this option can be annoying while you are working.

Bypass the other options in this dialog box. We shall discuss the more important ones later in this book.

■ Meeting the Office Assistants

Word 2000 puts at your disposal eight **Assistants** to help you. The Office Assistant is an interactive program.

The role of an **Assistant** is to answer your questions whenever you put them. To call an Assistant, click on the speech bubble containing a question mark, located in the upper right corner of your screen.

In the dialog box which appears, enter what you want to do. Once your question has been clearly entered, click on **Search**.

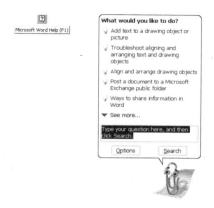

Figure 1.5 Click on the icon with the question mark to call up the Assistant.

You will see a number of bulleted items which list topics on actions connected with what you have asked.

Click on the one that matches what you want to do. If none of them matches, click on **See more...** at the end of the list.

A Help window will be displayed, which will contain the information required. Some keywords will be hyperlinks (in blue and underlined). Click on them and they will open explanations.

 *If you enter **Office Assistant** and click on the **Search** button, **Clippit** will ask you if you would like the help of an Office Assistant, change Assistant, hide, show, or turn off the assistant, and so on.*

If you wish to change Office Assistant or some of the related options, click on **Options**; the **Gallery** and **Options** tabs will appear (see Figure 1.6).

The **Gallery** options tab of the **Office Assistant** dialog box introduces you to Clippit, the paper clip, and the other Office

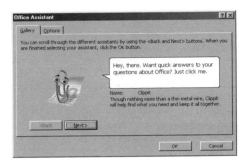

Figure 1.6: The Gallery tab allows you to view a series
of different Office Assistants.

Assistants. You may choose between the following Office
Assistants (see Figure 1.7):

- **Clippit**. General guide.
- **The Dot.**
- **F1**, the first of the 300/M series, built to serve.
- **The Genius**. He resembles Einstein.
- **Office Logo**.
- **Mother Nature**. She changes.
- **Links**. A cat that will never chase your mouse.
- **Rocky**. A computer guide dog.

Click on **Next** for a presentation of the Office Assistants.

Figure 1.7 The eight Office Assistants of Word 2000.

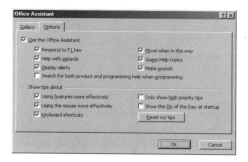

Figure 1.8 Making choices in the Options tab of the Office Assistants dialog.

The **Options** tab of the **Office Assistant** dialog box offers a series of check boxes, including:

- Respond to F1 key;
- Help with wizards;
- Display alerts;
- Move when in the way;
- Guess Help topics;
- Make sounds.

Tick the selections that best suit your personal requirements and click on **OK**.

Let us assume that you have chosen Clippit as your Office Assistant and called for help. Clippit starts by asking you what you want to do and invites you to take action (see Figure 1.5).

Clippit is full of advice, like an informed and conscientious teacher. When you have a specific question, enter a keyword for the question in the text panel, for example 'Tabs'. Clippit then offers you a choice of actions related to tab stops, on which you might wish to obtain information.

Click on the option that matches your requirement:

- set tab stops with leader characters;
- clear one or more tab stops;
- set tab stops;
- change spacing between default tab stops, and so on.

Let us assume that you would like to set some tab stops. The Office Assistant displays the Microsoft Word Help window showing the required information, together with some additional hints and tips.

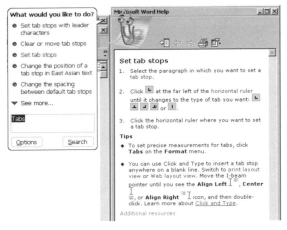

Figure 1.9 Clicking on an option makes the Office Assistant display the corresponding Help information.

 The Assistant is common to all Office applications. Any changes you make to it in Word will also apply in Excel or PowerPoint (and, the other way round, modifications made in Excel or PowerPoint will in turn apply in Word).

■ Viewing the screen

You have installed Word 2000. You have configured its basic features. You have started it, and a document with default formatting is displayed before you. Before starting work, familiarise yourself with the screen layout.

A cursor, an insertion point, pull-down menus, submenus, commands, options, buttons, icons, dialog boxes, mouse buttons, taskbar, title bar, menu bar, toolbar, status bar – which do what? What are they all used for?

Word 2000 displays each document in a window of its own. Each of these windows is a full Word application window, with its own Title bar, showing the Word icon, the document name and the application name – Microsoft Word.

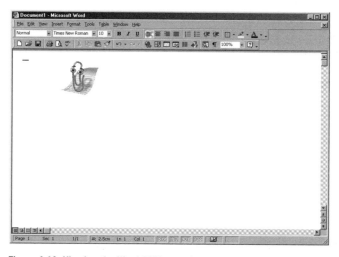

Figure 1.10 Viewing the Word 2000 new document screen.

Each of these Word 2000 application screens comprises five main parts:

- the **Title** bar;
- the **Menu** bar;
- the **Status** bar;
- the **Toolbar**(s);
- the **Document** window.

The Title bar

The **Title bar** is located at the top of the Word window.

On the left-hand side, it displays the application's icon, the name of the current document and the name of the application. Clicking on the icon opens a pull-down menu with the following options: **Restore, Move, Size, Minimize, Maximize** and **Close**.

On the right-hand side, it shows three buttons: **Minimize, Maximize/Restore** and **Close**).

Minimize   Close

Figure 1.11 The Title bar.

Restore /
Maximize

Buttons and menu entries fulfil the same functions:

- **To minimise a window.** Click on the **Minimize** button on the right of the Title bar. Alternatively, click on the **Word** icon on the left of the Title bar and select **Minimize** in the menu. This takes the window off the desktop and puts it as an entry on the Task bar at the bottom of your screen.

- **To maximise a window.** Click on the **Maximize** button on the right of the Title bar. Alternatively, click on the **Word** icon on the left of the Title bar and select **Maximize** in the menu. This makes the Word application window fill the entire desktop. The **Maximize** button on the right of the

Title bar changes name and appearance to become a **Restore** button.

- **To restore a window.** After minimising or maximising a window, you can restore it to its previous size and position on the screen as follows:
  - **After maximising.** Click on the **Restore** button on the right of the Title bar. Alternatively, click on the **Word** icon on the left of the Title bar and select **Restore** in the menu.
  - **After minimising.** Click on the window's entry in the **Task bar** at the bottom of your screen.

- **To switch between windows.** You can have several Word windows open simultaneously. To switch from one to the other, click on the corresponding entry in the **Task bar** at the bottom of your screen. Alternatively, you can switch from one to another by pressing **Ctrl+F6**.

- **To move a window.** Click anywhere in the Title bar and, with the left mouse button pressed, drag the whole application window to a different position on the screen.

- **To resize a window.** Position the mouse pointer on one of the borders or corners of the window until it changes into a bi-directional horizontal, vertical or diagonal arrow. Drag it, with the left mouse button depressed, to obtain the desired window size.

To be on the safe side... Before moving or resizing a window, you can click on the Word icon on the left of the Title bar and select **Move** *or* **Size** *in the menu. This changes the mouse pointer to a four-directional arrow which, when clicked outside a corner, border or the title bar, has no effect on the document.*

- **To close a window.** Click on the **Close** icon on the right of the Title bar. Alternatively, click on the **Word** icon on the left of the Title bar and select **Close** in the menu. Closing a window frees space on your screen and in your computer's memory.

The Menu bar

The **Menu bar** is located below the Title bar. It is composed of nine menus:

- File;
- Edit;
- View;
- Insert;
- Format;
- Tools;
- Table;
- Window;
- Help.

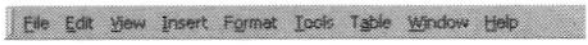

Figure 1.12 The Menu bar.

The Status bar

Together with the Title bar and the Menu bar, the **Status bar** is the third bar that you will always meet in Word 2000, even if all other bars and rulers are switched off and no document is open. The Status bar is located at the bottom of the applications window and displays various current parameter values:

- **Page** *number.* The page number of the page shown, based on the page numbers you gave the document, if any.
- **Sec** *number.* The section number of the page shown in the window.
- *Number/number.* The page number and the total number of pages based on the physical page count in the document.
- **At** *number.* The distance from the top of the page to your insertion point. No measurement is displayed if the insertion point is not in the window.

- **Ln** *number*. The line of text where the insertion point is located. No measurement is displayed if the insertion point is not in the window.

- **Col** *number*. The distance, in number of characters, from the left margin to the insertion point. No measurement is displayed if the insertion point is not in the window.

- **Command modes.**
    - **REC.** RECord macro mode.
    - **TRK.** TRacK changes mode.
    - **EXT.** EXTend selection mode.
    - **OVR.** OVeRtype mode.

- **Current language.** English (U.K.).

- **Status of the spelling checker.** A checkmark indicates that no spelling mistakes were found. Otherwise an 'X' appears.

Figure 1.13 The Status bar.

The toolbars

The toolbars are located below the Menu bar.

Figure 1.14 The toolbars.

There are a number of toolbars. Word 2000 allows you to customise them in two ways:

- by adding or removing tool buttons provided by default, available from the **Customize** dialog box of the **Tools** menu or via the **Add/remove buttons** function, accessible by clicking on the **More buttons** button of the toolbar in question;

Figure 1.16 The Customize dialog box and Toolbars tab.

- by creating your own toolbars or using existing toolbars to add tools you develop yourself with the aid of macros.

 Macros are recordings of key strokes, allowing repetitive actions to be automated. You program them yourself (see Chapter 4).

To customise your toolbars, perform the following:

1. Open the **Tools** menu.
2. Select the **Customize** option.
3. Click on the **Commands** tab.
4. Select a command category.
5. Scroll through the commands in the selected category.

Figure 1.17 Options for customising a toolbar.

6. Click on those which are of interest.

7. Drag them to your toolbar.

For each icon there is a corresponding explanatory **ScreenTip**. ScreenTips can be deactivated; here is how to proceed:

1. Open the **View** menu.

2. Select the **Toolbars** submenu.

3. Select the **Customize** option.

4. Click the **Options** tab in the **Customize** dialog box.

5. Clear the **Show ScreenTips** on the Toolbars check box.

The text entry area

Word 2000 displays each document in a separate application window, each with its own Title bar, menu bar, Toolbars, Status bar, and so on. The document window in a narrower sense, that is, the area where you type in your text and lay out your document, presents some more elements that help you with your work, such as rulers, scrollbars, view buttons and different shapes of cursor.

The ruler

How the ruler is displayed varies according to the viewing mode and the current location of the insertion point (normal text, columns or table).

Figure 1.18 The ruler shows the current tab stops.

In Normal and Print Layout view

In both **Normal** and **Print Layout** view, the ruler shows the indent markers and tab stops. The grey-coloured portions of the ruler represent the page margins. The current type of tabulation is displayed at the extreme left. Click on this button to change the type of tab stop.

▪ **Left tab** – text aligns to the left of the tab stop;

▪ **Center tab** – text is centred on the tab stop;

▪ **Right tab** – text aligns to the right of the tab stop;

▪ **Decimal tab** – numbers align on the decimal point.

Further clicks change this button to **Bar tab, First Line Indent** and **Hanging Indent** (ask your **Office Assistant** for a detailed description).

Click the ruler where you want to set a tab stop. If necessary, drag the tab stop to position it where you want it. To clear a tab stop, drag it from the ruler.

In Table view

When the insertion point is in a table, the ruler shows the column markers which you can click and drag to change column widths. Indent markers are shown for the currently active column.

The scroll bars

There are two scroll bars: one horizontal, at the bottom of the screen, and one vertical, on the right of the screen. To move up and down in the text, do the following:

Figure 1.19 The cursor is pointing to the vertical scroll bar.

- to scroll up one line, click the up scroll arrow;
- to scroll down one line, click the down scroll arrow;
- to scroll up one screen, click above the scroll box;
- to scroll down one screen, click below the scroll box;
- to scroll to a specific page, drag the scroll box.

Figure 1.20 The cursor is pointing to the horizontal scroll bar.

To move left and right in the text, click the left or right scroll arrow or drag the scroll box of the horizontal scroll bar.

The cursors

The cursor is one of the most important working tools. It is the visual representation of the mouse on the screen. It can take different forms according to its current operation and environment.

By default, the cursor is arrow-shaped. Some software utilities can create animated cursors (pen, galloping horse, dinosaur and so on). Such programs are available in shops or on the Internet.

The **Text cursor** lets you set the insertion point anywhere in the text. It is shaped like an I. Click in any desired location to set the insertion point. Select text by keeping the mouse button pressed: the text appears highlighted (white letters on a black background).

Figure 1.21 The text insertion point.

To activate the **drag-and-drop** function, perform the following steps:

1. Select the word to be moved.
2. Keep the mouse button depressed.
3. Drag the word you wish to move. The cursor is changed into a white arrow at the centre of a small grey rectangle. This drag-and-drop cursor indicates that the selection (word or phrase) will be moved.

Figure 1.22 The drag-and-drop cursor.

In **Print Preview** view, the cursor becomes a **magnifying glass**. You can use it to enlarge the screen. Once in Print Preview view, select the magnifying glass icon and click the text to be enlarged. This function allows you to see exactly how the printed page will appear.

Figure 1.23 The magnifying glass cursor.

The **Resizing cursor** serves for moving the margins in **Print Preview** mode. It takes the form of a double-pointed arrow when placed on the ruler.

Figure 1.24 The Resizing cursor.

The **Split cursor** appears when setting split-bars. Placed on a split-bar, the cursor changes to a double-headed vertical arrow.

Figure 1.25 The Split cursor.

The **Outline cursor** can move elements in **Outline View** mode. It is a cross covered by four arrowheads. In Outline view, it permits the block selection of text attached to a heading level, by clicking on the cross located to the left of the heading.

Figure 1.26 The Outline cursor.

The **Help pointer** has the form of a normal cursor, with a question mark. You can obtain it by selecting the What's This? option on the Help menu.

Figure 1.27 The Help pointer.

Having selected this command, you lead the pointer to a keyword or some area of the screen you would like to have explained. An explanation then appears in a large balloon.

For example, if you lead the Help pointer to the scroll bar, and click on the left mouse button, you will obtain a fairly detailed response.

Don't worry! In the following lessons you will have the opportunity of learning these functions in practice.

■ Using a dialog box

Dialog boxes are designed to give you full, sometimes exhaustive, information on a given subject. They comprise various tabs which are accessed by clicking on their titles.

Figure 1.29 The Break dialog box with radio buttons and command buttons.

- **Tabs.** These are arranged like tabbed cards in an index.
- **Radio buttons.** These allow an option to be selected.
- **Check boxes.** These are activated by a simple click with the left mouse button.
- **Text boxes.** You use them to enter text or numerical data.
- **Scroll lists.** These present lists of options for you to choose from by clicking.

- **Counters.** These are small boxes with arrows for raising or lowering a numerical value.

- **Command buttons.** These allow commands to be validated or cancelled.

- **Closure box.** A button marked by a multiplication sign. It is located at the top right-hand corner of each box. Clicking one closes that particular active dialog.

2 Creating a document

■ Starting the easy way

When Word 2000 starts up, the screen is ready for use. Any characters typed will appear immediately on the screen. For this chapter, we shall use a text extracted from a holiday guide on bird watching. We are going to begin with the title.

Insertion point and end marker

Two reference markers are there to guide you when you start writing. Firstly, a vertical line, about half a centimetre long, blinking. This marks the place where the next letter will be inserted and is called the insertion point. As you type, it moves to the right.

The second reference marker is a fixed horizontal line, about the same length as the blinking vertical line. This line is always positioned at the beginning of the last line of the text. When you type several lines of text, it moves downwards.

Figure 2.1 The insertion point, the start of your text.

Click and Type

The new Click and Type tool ought to facilitate tasks which were difficult in previous versions. For example, faced with an empty white page, you could not type text straight in the middle of the page. You had to begin at the top of the page or insert some blank lines. You can now begin typing any-where on the page, but certain conditions apply. The screen must be in **Print Layout** view (**View** menu, **Print Layout** option). Click and Type is not available when working in multiple columns.

This mode facilitates tidiness and helps to save time. Now your work page will look more like a piece of paper and less like a data processing screen. In Click and Type mode the cursor takes a form adapted to its position (as shown in the Help windows in Figure 2.2). For insertions into an already typed location, Click and Type adopts by default the style of the current paragraph.

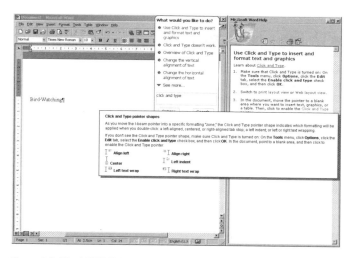

Figure 2.2 Word 2000 Help information about the Click and Type method.

Giving the text a heading

Type in Bird Watching. As you type, the insertion point moves to the right.

After writing Bird Watching, jump several lines by pressing the **Enter** key a few times.

The horizontal end of text marker moves downwards. You have just introduced some line breaks. All line breaks are connected to the action of pressing the Enter key. They form an intentional break in the text, and are to be used only to separate one block from another.

Up to now, the insertion point and end of text marker have been located on the same line. At the start, they were almost touching. Progressively, the insertion point moves to the right, while the end of text marker remains stationary at the left-hand edge. Now, four or five lines lower down, the two markers are again side by side.

■ Writing a paragraph

To write the first paragraph, it is necessary to move the insertion point back upwards. To do this, press the Up arrow key. The insertion point moves up. Position it two lines below the heading.

You can now type in the whole paragraph (see Figure 2.3). However, your text does not have a very finished look. We will take care of its formatting later.

This is the most effective and quickest way to proceed. For now, be content to type in text 'as you go'.

Automatic line wrapping

While keying in text, you need not worry about line breaks. These are automatic.

Figure 2.3 Text entry.

Selecting a viewing mode

After writing the heading and first paragraph, you have a provisionally coherent presentation. In Word 2000, Normal mode is the best adapted for simple typing.

If you want to change the way in which Word 2000 displays your text, click **View** on the Menu bar. An pull-down menu appears, with a range of options and commands. Try them one by one:

- **Normal.** The default document view for the majority of word processing jobs (typing in, editing, formatting and so on). Normal mode is often used for straightforward typing.

- **Web Layout.** This option is ideal for displaying and reading documents on the screen. In this mode, Word 2000 displays in the same manner as Windows Explorer, which gives quick access to different parts of your document.

Figure 2.4 Normal mode is the best adapted to straightforward typing.

- **Print Layout.** This option shows how your page will look
  when printed on paper. This mode makes heavy demands
  on memory and can slow document scrolling.

- **Outline.** This option allows you to work on the document
  structure. This is the mode you should use for organising
  and developing the document contents.

Choose the one which suits you best. Outline mode is complex
and is not suited to the simple preliminary work of document
creation.

Viewing mode selection buttons

An alternative way to switch between viewing modes is con-
stituted by four selection buttons which, in all four views, are
located at the bottom left corner of the screen, directly above
the status bar.

Figure 2.5 The four selection buttons for the different viewing modes are located at the bottom of the screen.

In the context of this exercise, choose **Print Layout** view. The two rulers serve as points of reference and allow margins to be set (you will learn how later).

Figure 2.6 The Print Layout view displays two rulers.

 The rulers allow you to locate objects and to change paragraph indents, margins and other layout parameters.

■ Navigating within the text

When keying in text, it often needs correcting. Whether it is a question of changes, deletions or additions, the first step is to position the insertion point at the place where the intervention is desired.

There are two types of movement: moving and scrolling.

Moving

Moving is done with the aid of the mouse or the keyboard. To move the insertion point with the mouse, simply click at any point for that instantly to become the active point in the text.

Alternatively, there are keyboard shortcuts which will move the cursor as follows.

⬅	One character to the left.
➡	One character to the right.
⬆	One line upwards.
⬇	One line downwards.
Ctrl + ➡	One word to the right.
Ctrl + ⬅	One word to the left.

For the following moves, the digits must be typed on the numeric keypad.

⇧ + 7	Move to the start of the line.
⇧ + 1	Move to the end of the line.
⇧ + 3	Move one window depth downwards.
⇧ + 9	Move one window depth upwards.
Ctrl + Alt + Pg⬇	Move one page downwards.
Ctrl + Alt + Pg⬆	Move one page upwards.
Ctrl + 7	Move to the start of the document.
Ctrl + 1	Move to the end of the document.

Scrolling

Scrolling is done using the mouse. There are two types of scroll bars: one horizontal and one vertical. To scroll the screen up and down, just click with the mouse on one of the two black arrows located at the extreme right of your screen.

Select Browse Object (Alt+Ctrl+Home)

Figure 2.7 The vertical scroll bar with the Browse button.

Scrolling can also be done by specific item. To achieve this, click on the button located at the bottom of the vertical scroll bar between the two double arrow buttons. A mini-screen appears containing 12 boxes with the options shown below.

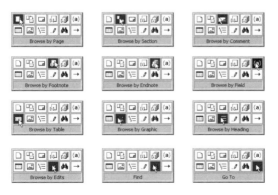

Figure 2.8 The 12 options available after pressing the Browse button.

Figure 2.9 If you do not need the Browse
button after all, just cancel it.

Having made your selection, Browse by Graphic for example,
click on the round button with the mouse. Your text scrolls,
graphic by graphic.

One other function, available in all views, provides an indi-
cation of the pages being browsed while scrolling.

Let's say that the text covers a dozen pages and that you need
to make a change on page 7: you need only drag the vertical
scroll box with the mouse in order to reach a given page
number.

Figure 2.10 The Info-balloon shows the page number.

■ Editing text

The Clipboard

Word 2000 uses the **Clipboard** utility. This allows you to
store bits of documents, whole documents even, or pictures.
You can restore them later elsewhere in the document or in
another application.

The Word 2000 clipboard can hold 12 different items, and
for an indeterminate period.

Cut-and-paste a word

There are two ways of moving text:

- The first is common to all applications that run under Windows: it uses the cut-and-paste or copy-and-paste methods with the clipboard.

- The second is drag-and-drop.

Cut-and-paste means cutting out the selected text (which is then transferred to the clipboard) for insertion into a different location of the document. The 'cut' action can be effected via the keyboard using the key combination **Ctrl+X** or by clicking on the **Cut** command in the **Edit** menu. Here's how it's done:

1. Select a word by double-clicking on it. It then appears highlighted in black. In our example, the word 'Bird' is no longer displayed in black on white, but in white on a black background.

2. Click on **Edit** in the menu bar.

3. Click on **Cut**. The word then disappears from the screen.

4. Using the mouse, select an insertion point.

5. Click on **Edit** again.

6. Click on **Paste**. The word is inserted at your chosen location.

You can also use the **Shift+Ins** keyboard shortcut to paste the word at the new location. The text to the right of the insertion point is displaced automatically. The line breaks are reorganised by Word 2000 and the text is run in smoothly at the insertion point.

Copy-and-paste a word

To copy a word, a phrase, a paragraph or a text, perform the following:

1. Select the part to be copied.

Figure 2.11 The Paste command on the Edit drop-down menu.

2. Open the **Edit** menu.

3. Select **Copy** . The word or text is copied to the **Clipboard**.

4. Place the insertion point at the desired location.

5. Click on **Paste**.

Drag-and-drop a word

In the following example, we are going to show you how to relocate a word on a sentence using the drag-and-drop method.

1. Select the phrase segment 'Bird watching' with the mouse.

2. Position the mouse cursor within the selection and click, keeping the mouse button depressed until the cursor takes the form of an arrow, the head pointing upwards to the left.

3. The selection is ready to be moved by the mouse.

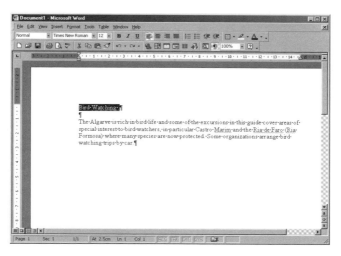

Figure 2.12 The drag-and-drop method.

4. Still keeping the button depressed, drag the selection to its new location.

   During the move, the cursor takes the form of a small rectangle, below the arrow.

5. At the new location, release the mouse button. The selected text is inserted and everything returns to normal.

Undo and Redo a command

When you modify text, it is not unusual to change your mind and want to undo an action and go back to how things were. You have just moved a word to a place which is not appropriate. All you have to do is undo the action by selecting the **Undo-move** button.

Word 2000 permits more than 1000 levels of Undo. You can also change your mind again and reverse an Undo change. Therefore, losing data should become a very rare event.

Figure 2.13 The Undo-move button.

Ctrl+Z to Undo an action

To reverse an action, another way of proceeding is to use the **Ctrl** (Control) key, and keep it depressed while pressing the Z key. The **Ctrl+Z** key combination reverses the last action. If you press Ctrl+Z once, the change you have just made disappears.

Ctrl+Y to Redo an action

If you now press the **Ctrl+Y** (Redo) combination, the last Undo change is reversed. If you press Ctrl+Y again, the change reoccurs. The Undo and Redo actions have been performed in an 'intelligent' manner. Word 2000 has noted your actions in logical steps. It does not work character by character.

■ Correcting text

After entering some text, you can check your spelling and grammar as follows:

1. Open the **Tools** menu.
2. Click on the **Spelling and Grammar** command, or click on the **ABC** button, which is usually to be found next to the **Print Preview** button (magnifying glass motif) on the **Standard** toolbar.

Correcting spelling mistakes is relatively easy. Just follow the suggested corrections which appear. You can accept suggestions, ignore them or add new words to the dictionary. These will be recognised in future just like the initial dictionary entries.

In the text presented to the spelling and grammar checker, Word has underlined 'Marim', which is not in the dictionary, because this is the name of a not very well known place.

Your first reaction should be to add the word Marim to the Word dictionary. This is useful if you know that this word will appear several times in your text.

On the other hand, since this is not a proper dictionary entry, you may decide for yourself whether or not to add it to the Word dictionary. If you do not wish to add it to the dictionary, just click on the **Ignore** command button.

If you have made a mistake by adding an extra space before a word, the checker marks it immediately and asks if you wish to change it. When you validate this request by clicking on the **Change** button, the extra space is removed.

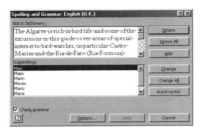

Figure 2.14 Your text in the Spelling and Grammar checker.

Details of the new checkers

In comparison to Word 97, Word 2000 offers improvements to the spelling and grammar checking function. The library of proper nouns includes the names of countries, towns, various organisations and societies, as well as of famous people. If, by chance, certain stars of screen or stage are not yet listed there, the Add command of the spelling and grammar checker lets you remedy the omission.

For your guidance, be aware that the dictionary may not contain names of the latest pop groups, and so, for example, if you type 'Boyzone' it will mark it as wrong, and suggest replacing it with 'Boy zone'. This feature may have some

Figure 2.15 The grammar checker in action. It offers to correct poor grammar, here a double negative.

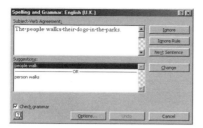

Figure 2.16 Suggestions for alternative subject–verb agreement for the present tense.

quirks, as, for example, it does not recognise Princess Di, suggesting instead 'Did, Die, Dig, Dim, Din, Dip, Dib, Do, Dui'.

The grammar checker offers grammatical rules presented clearly and simply (see Figures 2.15 and 2.16). It is, therefore, usable by everyone, which was not the case with previous versions. It can be permanently active. It can also, according to the mode of use options settings, change every occurrence of a false term within the body of a text in whatever variation of the term it occurs.

■ Multiple insertions: a 12–item Clipboard

Apart from the traditional copy and paste commands, which are unchanged, Word 2000 offers a notable improvement. It concerns the users who insert numerous objects into their documents. The new Clipboard in Word 2000 is common to all Office 2000 applications: Excel, Microsoft Access, Microsoft Outlook and PowerPoint. It can hold up to 12 different items: text, pictures, or any other object that can be copied and pasted. Traditional clipboards can be used in any application to perform copy operations, but only Office 2000 applications support the use of the new model Clipboard. In

Figure 2.17 To use the new Clipboard, its toolbar must be displayed.

its current version, the contents of each cache cannot be viewed. That limits its utilisation since it is necessary to remember the contents of each item. For the moment, clicking the right mouse button does not allow a preview. When the content is a text, the help balloon displays the start of the text. For pictures, only the Item 1, Item 2… label is shown.

To use the Clipboard, click first on the **Toolbars** option of the **View** menu, then select **Clipboard**. The clipboard cells are presented in lines of four, with extra lines added as and when necessary.

The menu options allow you to make an insertion in the Clipboard, paste one or all of the items or empty the Clipboard completely.

Figure 2.18 Multiple insertions, thanks to 12-item storage in the clipboard common to Office applications.

■ Save or Save As

Choose a drive

Once your text has been entered and corrected, you should save it in a directory or subdirectory. You must first decide on which drive you want to create your directory, the **C:** drive or the **D:** drive? Let's assume you decide on the **C:** drive. In this case, you have to create a directory on the C: disk.

1. Access Windows Explorer.

2. Once there, select the **C:** drive.

Figure 2.19 Click on Windows Explorer.

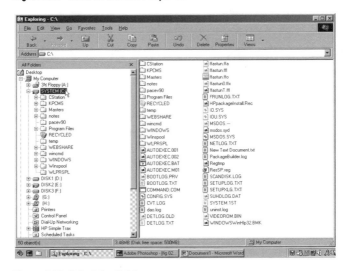

Figure 2.20 Select the C drive.

To choose a directory

1. Open the **File** menu after selecting the C: drive.
2. Select **New**.
3. Select the **Folder** option.

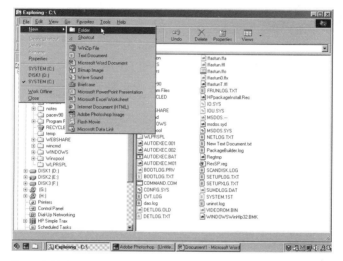

Figure 2.21 Create a new folder.

We need only enter a name in the name box. Incidentally, by what name do you want to call your Bird Watching file? Here again, choose the most descriptive name possible. Let's suppose that you choose the name Bird Watching, your directory immediately relocates itself in the C: drive directory tree in alphabetical order.

To choose a subdirectory

If you are methodical, you can similarly create a subdirectory and give it a name. Call it 'Leisure Activities' and put your

Figure 2.22 The Leisure Activities subdirectory is located in the Bird Watching directory on your C: drive.

file in it. To do this, open the **File** menu, click on the **Save** command and specify the Leisure Activities subdirectory which is located in the Bird Watching directory of the **C:** drive.

It is recommended that you **Save** your work every five or ten minutes, so as not to lose any work done in the time interval.

Giving your file a name
Up to now your file has had a name only by default. It is called Document1.

It is preferable to give it a more descriptive name to avoid confusion. The proliferation of files called Document 1, 2, 3, 4, 5, 6... would eventually become totally confusing.

Word automatically numbers new documents in sequential order (Document1, Document2 and so on) and continues this number sequence even if the previous document has been closed.

1. Select a title for your file, for example, Bird Watching.
2. Open the **File** menu.
3. Select the **Save As** command.
4. In the name field at the bottom of the dialog box, enter your chosen name, which in this case is Bird Watching.

   Word 2000 suggests the extension .doc. However, several other formats are available. This allows you to share files with other users (Macintosh, for example) or any other standard text formats on the market. To select one of them, click on the scrolled list, on the line which lists that format by default.

   To recapitulate: **C:\Bird Watching\Leisure Activities\Bird Watching.doc**

You now know how to enter text, to edit it, to check it for grammar and spelling, to give it a name and store it in a folder. You have just created your first document.

3 Formatting a page

Formatting a document page consists of applying normal methods of presentation but adding a personal touch. It is a question of refining the look of the page. To do this, various parameters come into play: aligning the text, setting indents, applying a suitable character font, adding page breaks, page headers and footers, finding an original border, decorating the text with one or two dropped initials: there is no shortage of possibilities.

■ Aligning text

Text in a document can be left-aligned, right-aligned, centred or justified. Left-aligned is the Word 2000 default alignment. For each form of alignment there is a button on the **Formatting** toolbar:

Figure 3.1 The text alignment buttons.

- **Left-aligned** text is aligned down the left margin, but is uneven, or ragged, at the right margin. You can use this style for private correspondence, for example, where a degree of informality is in order.

- **Right-aligned** text is flush with the right margin and uneven at the left margin. This type of alignment is useful for lists, or when numbering pages.

- **Centred** text is set evenly between the two margins. It is best for titles and headings, and also for poetry.

- **Justified** text is aligned with both margins. It creates the tidy look often used in newspapers and official documents.

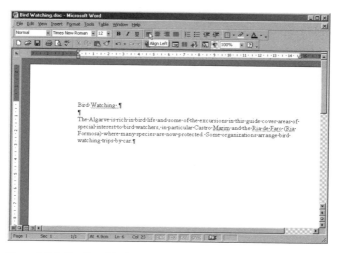

Figure 3.2 Left-aligned text.

■ Setting indents

Using the ruler, indents are easily set. The ruler carries indent markers shaped like small triangles. You can slide them right or left on the ruler.

A negative indent pulls the first line in a paragraph towards the left to distinguish it from the rest of the paragraph. Negative indents are used essentially for enumerations, bulleted lists, bibliography entries, or numbered sections in a curriculum vitae.

 Do not confuse the setting of paragraph indents with the definition of the left or right margins! Paragraph indents are measured from the margin lines, not from the paper edges. Margin settings define the blank spaces left around the text.

Modifying the first line indent

On the graduated ruler, the small triangle pointing downwards is the indent marker for the first line of a paragraph. The indent can be to the left (negative indent) or to the right (positive indent).

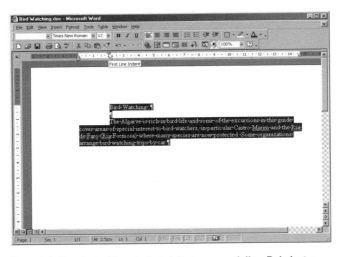

Figure 3.3 Your text with an indented first paragraph line. To indent a whole document, press Ctrl+A first to select all the text.

Changing the paragraph indent

On the graduated ruler, the small upwards pointing triangle is the left paragraph indent marker.

Another way of proceeding is to select the **Format** menu, choose the **Paragraph** option and click on the Indents and Spacing tab.

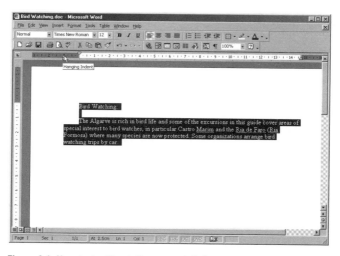

Figure 3.4 Your text with a left paragraph indent.

Note that, to apply an alignment to the whole of a text, the whole text must first be selected (with **Ctrl+A** or by clicking on the **Select All** command on the **Edit** menu).

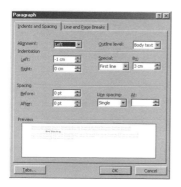

Figure 3.5 The Indents and Spacing tab in the Paragraph dialog box.

■ Cutting text

Nothing is more annoying than to see an item of text spread over two pages when the second page only contains a single line. These stray lines are known as widows and orphans.

Avoiding widows and orphans

The **Widow/Orphan** control option is on the **Line and Page Breaks** tab of the **Format/Paragraph** dialog box. This option makes reading a text a much more fluid process.

Keep lines together

Still on the subject of page formatting, the **Keep lines together** option means that lines in a paragraph will not be separated.

Let's say that your paragraph comprises some 20 lines and that the available space on your page is about 10 lines; if the Keep lines together option is activated, the whole of the paragraph will be carried over to the next page.

For this option, select the **Format** menu, choose the **Paragraph** submenu, click the **Lines and Page Breaks** tab and check the **Keep lines together** box.

Figure 3.6 The Keep lines together option in the Paragraph dialog box.

Keep with next

The **Keep with next** option prohibits a page break after a paragraph. This is a very useful function if, for example, you want to keep a chart and its caption together.

■ Applying borders and frames

There are numerous ways to use borders and frames. You can place borders around pages, phrases, words, pictures and tables, and also create a basic frame in the colour of your choice. All that adds up to a plus for your page formatting. Be careful not to go over the top – you can have too much of a good thing!

Borders

To apply a border to a whole text, or paragraph by paragraph, choose the **Format/Borders and Shading** command.

There are different types of border:

Box   Shadow

3-D   Custom

There are also different styles of border:

- continuous;
- dotted.

Twenty-four types of line are offered in nine thicknesses and fourty colours.

Borders and shading for pages and paragraphs

Word 2000 offers some 150 new borders. Amongst them are several borders in 3-D and frames intended for the publication

Bird·Watching·¶
¶
The·Algarve·is·rich·in·bird·life·and·some·of·the·excursions·in·this·guide·cover·areas·of·
special·interest·to·bird·watchers,·in·particular·Castro·Marim·and·the·Ria·de·Faro·(Ria·
Formosa)·where·many·species·are·now·protected·.Some·organizations·arrange·bird·
watching·trips·by·car.¶

Figure 3.7 A border applied to a paragraph.

of brochures or small papers. Page borders are enhanced by contributions from Microsoft Publisher, just like the improvements in Web page publication which, as we will see later, are strongly linked to FrontPage. In fact, these products are more or less intermixed, to the benefit of Word 2000 users.

From now on, you can apply borders not only to whole pages, but also to parts of text or text boxes. The same goes for shading which can apply, if you want, to just a single word.

Borders can also be applied to each side of a page. Pay attention, however, to their application. They do not always work as you might intend. In fact, if you select a number of lines to frame, you will obtain, with the border tool, as many frames as there are line breaks. In a list, you will obtain as many frames as there are elements in the list. To avoid this unwanted effect, perform the following:

1. Create a table cell.

2. Cut what you wish to frame.

3. Adjust the cell width.

4. Click in the cell.

5. Paste the text to be framed.

By doing this, the text framed in the cell adapts in width to the size of it, and not the other way round.

Shading a word or a sequence of words

To add emphasis to a paragraph, a word or a sequence of words, proceed as follows:

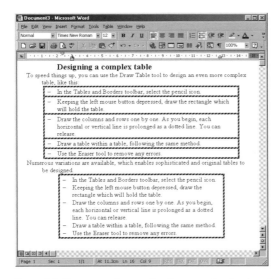

Figure 3.8 Two ways of presenting frames using borders. In the second case, a cell is created which is resized later.

1. Make your selection.
2. Open the **Format** menu and then select the **Borders and Shading** submenu.
3. In the dialog box which appears, select a colour or a grey. In the example, we have chosen a Grey-10% shade.
4. Click **OK**.

Frame

It is possible, at any time, to apply a frame or a background colour to a selected paragraph. Various combinations of colours and shadings (background or foreground) are available. In the following example, we have chosen a Grey-40%.

Bird Watching.

The Algarve is rich in bird life and some of the excursions in this guide cover areas of special interest to bird watches, in particular Castro Marim and the Ria de Faro (Ria Formosa) where many species are now protected. Some organizations arrange bird watching trips by car.

Boat Services.

There is a boat service from Vila Real to Ayamonte in Spain. It operates 24 hours a day from 1 June to 30 September and also at Christmas. The rest of the year it runs from 0700 to 2300 (0800 to midnight Spanish time). There are boats from Faro out to its beaches, from Olhao to the islands of Culatra and Armona, from the Tavira to Ilha de Tavira.

Figure 3.9 A grey background frame applied to a selected paragraph.

■ Numbering paragraphs

Numbered or bulleted lists allow you to generate lists very easily:

1. Enter the list without any numbers.

2. Select this list.

3. Click on the **Bullets** button on the **Formatting** toolbar.

To change the bullet symbol (even after the list has been completed):

1. Open the **Format** menu.

2. Click on the **Bullets and Numbering** command.

3. Select the **Bulleted** tab in the **Bullets and Numbering** dialog box.

Equally you could choose a number format and proceed to the offered options.

 It is possible to renumber a list by clicking on the button a second time. Incidentally, lists can be used in the cells of a table.

The procedure is identical to that for numbers, but it is possible to choose any character from one of the available fonts.

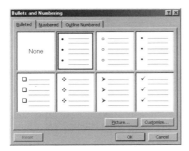

Figure 3.10 Click on the Bulleted tab in the Bullets and Numbering
dialog box to choose a bullet format.

■ Selecting a font

With Windows 95, you have the benefit of TrueType fonts.
These have the advantage of displaying as they will print.
They can be printed by all printers. The TrueType label is
abbreviated to TT at the side of each font name.

The default font in Word is Times New Roman. It is used in
new documents created from the active normal template.
Obviously, depending on the text, one font will be more suitable than another.

Selecting a font

You have the choice between the **Font...** option in the **Format**
menu, and the drop-down list of fonts on the Formatting
toolbar.

You can choose the font before or after writing the text. The
former is more logical.

1. Open the **Format** menu.
2. Click on the **Font...** option.

3. In the Font dialog box, select the **Font** tab.

4. Scroll the list of fonts.

5. Click on the one that suits you.

6. Confirm your choice with the **OK** button.

Changing a character font

To change a character font, use the menu or the toolbar. The procedure is the same as for choosing a character font: you select your text and then use the **Formatting** toolbar or the **Format** menu on the **Standard** toolbar.

To enlarge or reduce the font size

- Click on the **Font Size** drop-down arrow on the Formatting toolbar.
- Click on a new point size.

■ Adding emphasis

Text can be emphasised in the following manner:

1. Open the **Edit** menu.

2. Click on the **Select all** command. Your text is selected.

3. Open the **Format** menu.

4. Select the **Font** option.

5. In the **Font** dialog box, click on the **Font** tab.

6. Select one of the following **Font style** options:
  - Regular;
  - Italic;
  - Bold;
  - Bold Italic.

Word 2000 offers a quick way to emphasise text by enclosing a word, an expression or a phrase by conventional symbols. For example, to put the word 'exceptional' in bold, you type *exceptional*, to italicise it, you type _exceptional_ and so on. The marker symbols which encase the term disappear once the emphasis has been carried out.

Font effects

There are also other ways of enriching text: putting it into relief, or adding capital letters combined with various decorative effects. To access these options, perform the following:

1. Open the **Format** menu.
2. Click on the **Font** option.
3. In the **Font** dialog box, choose the **Font** tab.
4. Tick the enhancement boxes in the **Effects** area.

The principal options available are:

- **Strikethrough.** Draws a line through the selected text.
- **Double strikethrough.** Draws a double line through the selected text.
- **Shadow.** Adds a shadow behind the selected text, beneath and to the right of the text.
- **Outline.** Displays the inner and outer borders of each character.
- **Emboss.** Makes selected text appear as if it is raised off the page in relief.
- **Engrave.** Makes selected text appear as though printed or pressed into the page.
- **Small caps.** Formats selected lower case text as capitals and reduces their size. Small caps formatting does not affect numbers, punctuation, non-alphabetic characters or upper case letters.

Further options include **Superscript** and **Subscript** (as used, for example, in m^2 and H$_2$O), **All caps** and **Hidden**.

The Highlight option can be used to emphasise text. Click on the Highlight button (marker icon) in the Formatting toolbar, then select the text or object to highlight. When finished, click again on the button to deselect it. To change the marker colour, click on the drop-down arrow beside the Highlight button.

Dropped initial letter

To insert a dropped capital at the start of your text, perform the following:

1. Select the first capital letter of your paragraph.
2. Open the **Format** menu.
3. Select the **Drop Cap...** option.
4. Click on the **Dropped** option.
5. Confirm your choice with the **OK** button.

Figure 3.11 The Drop Cap dialog box of the Format menu.

Your selected capital changes shape to a dropped capital.

A dropped capital is usually the first letter of a paragraph. It can be displayed in the left margin or within the paragraph body in line with the left margin.

Figure 3.12 A dropped capital can improve the appearance of your text.

Case

Changing case means going from upper to lower case, or vice versa. To change case:

1. Open the **Format** menu.
2. Select the **Change Case...** option.
3. In the **Change Case** dialog box, tick the box with the option you prefer.
4. Confirm your choice with the **OK** button.

You can even change a whole text to upper or lower case.

Figure 3.13 The Change Case dialog box of the Format menu.

■ Setting margins

Preview your text to gain a good idea of how it will look when printed:

1. Open the **View** menu.
2. Select **Print Preview**. You can also click on the button representing a sheet of paper and a magnifying glass.
3. Both margin rulers are displayed.

   The Print Preview allows you to see immediately if the text is too high on the page. In that case you must change the top margin.
4. Slide the cursor over the top margin limit on the graduated ruler at the left of the screen.

   The cursor changes to a double-headed arrow which you can slide, holding the left mouse button depressed, to set the size of the top margin.

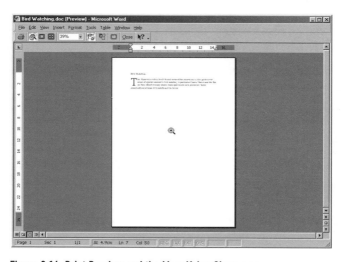

Figure 3.14 Print Preview and the Magnifying Glass cursor.

You can also set the margins in **Page Layout** view from the View menu.

1. Click on the margin limit of the appropriate graduated ruler.
2. When the cursor changes to a double-headed arrow, use it to slide the margin to the new setting.

■ Defining headers and footers

To define headers and footers for your document pages, perform the following:

1. Open the **View** menu.
2. Choose the **Header and Footer** option. A text zone labelled Header appears. You can enter headings as you wish, such as a document sub-title.

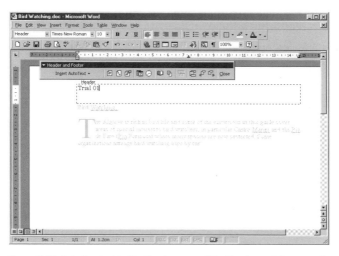

Figure 3.15 Entering text in the Header area of the Header and Footer option.

3. Enter the sub-title Trial 01.

4. Now click on the **Switch Between Header and Footer** button.

Figure 3.16 The Switch between Header and Footer button.

You are shown the Footer area, where you can enter, for example, page numbers, and/or the date, time and so on.

■ Displaying page numbers

This function is very useful when you write documents covering dozens of pages, such as reports or novels.

To display the current page number with the total number of pages, perform the following:

1. Open the **View** menu.

2. Click on **Header and Footer**. The header appears.

3. Click on the **Switch Between Header and Footer** button.

4. Go to the **Footer** area.

5. Open the **Insert AutoText** drop-down list on the **Header and Footer** toolbar.

6. Select the **Page X of Y** option. If your document contains 2 pages, the footer of page 1 shows Page 1 of 2. You can centre-align this pagination if you wish.

 Page numbers are automatically updated when you add or remove pages.

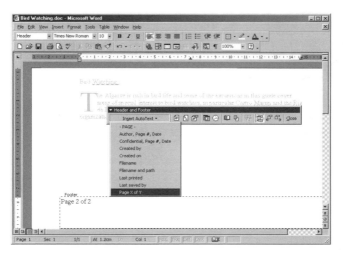

Figure 3.17 The Page X of Y automatic insert.

■ Applying the date and time to a document

This is a useful function, because it allows the last revision date of the document to be known.

The method used is similar to that used in the preceding pagination exercise:

1. Open the **View** menu.
2. Click on the **Header and Footer** option.
3. Switch from the header to the footer area.
4. Click on the **Insert Time** button (clock icon). The system time is inserted automatically.
5. Click on the **Insert Date** button (two calendar pages icon). The system date is inserted automatically.

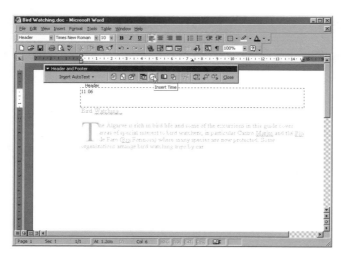

Figure 3.18 The Insert Time button inserts an automatically updated time field.

Finally, still in the footer area, click on the icon representing two calendar pages in order to insert the day's date.

4
Creating style sheets and templates

■ Choosing a style sheet

You have just written a document of some 200 pages. You have used the Times New Roman font, single line spacing, two lines between paragraphs and 14 point bold headings, but your boss wants you to use the Arial font, double line spacing, a single line between paragraphs and bold headings.

Everything needs changing! Over 200 pages, the job could become tedious. However, style sheets let you carry it out successfully in a few moments.

What is a style sheet?

A style sheet comprises a collection of styles, presented in a scrolled list box. A style comprises all the characteristics of a paragraph (indent measurements, alignment, borders, font and so on) collected together under a single name. Applying a style to a paragraph automatically endows it with all the characteristics of that style.

The same can be done for text in a document, since you do not use the same style for a figure caption, body text, a heading, a sub-heading, and so on. These can all have styles applied for font, point size, bold, italic, underline, and so on.

You have just written a standard type letter. Now apply different styles to it. The structure of your letter is as follows:

Laura Gibson Perfect Printing
22, Believer's Place
Sheffield S9 3QS

Dodgy Equipment Ltd
19, High Cost Lane
Swindon S39

Sheffield, 26 January 1999

Subject: Meeting of 19th February 1999

Dear Sir

Further to my telephone conversation with John Sinclair, may I ask you to arrange a meeting re: replacing your faulty equipment, on Wednesday 19th February at your headquarters in Swindon?

This meeting will hopefully bring to an end the lengthy discussions we have been having since last September and will allow our company to use the equipment for commercial purposes, as it was always intended.

It would be useful if you could invite one of your Senior Technicians as an expert.

We are bringing our own Senior Technician with a full report.

Hoping you will be able to confirm by return.

Yours sincerely

Laura Gibson
Managing Director

This letter comprises eleven paragraphs:

- the address of the addressee and the writer;
- the date;
- the subject;
- the text itself composed of 7 paragraphs;
- the closure.

The seven paragraphs in the body of the letter have an identical format. The four other paragraphs have different formats.

You are going to create different styles for these seven paragraphs. In total this will amount to what is called the style sheet. When you have created your style sheet, all you need to do when you write another letter is apply one of the styles to each new paragraph.

If you subsequently want to make modifications to your letter, you will only need to modify the appropriate style and all the paragraphs in that style will be modified automatically.

■ Creating a style sheet

To create a style sheet, you must define each style, that is to say, give it form and a name.

Using the toolbar

1. Select the address.
2. Click on the **Style** box located at the extreme left of the Formatting toolbar.

   This box contains a scrolled list of style names. By default, you will find Normal, Heading 1, Heading 2, Heading 3, Hyperlink and Default Paragraph Font.

3. In the text box, write the name that you want to give to the address style, for example Ad. From now on, you need only apply the style Ad to a section in order for its font, point size, and position on the page to be determined and consistent.
4. Proceed in the same way for the other elements of the letter.

Figure 4.1 The scrolled list of styles.

Using the dialog box

1. Select the element of the letter to which you want to attribute a style.

2. Open the **Format** menu.

3. Select **Style**. A dialog box appears on the screen. It contains the list of styles contained in your letter. The style you have just created also figures in the list.

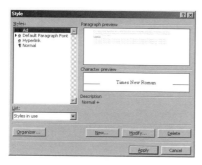

Figure 4.2 The Style dialog box.

You may choose between the following options:

- **New**. Create a new paragraph or character style.
- **Modify**. Modifies the selected style.
- **Delete**. Deletes the selected style.

4. Click on **New**. A new dialog box is displayed.

5. In the area entitled **Name**, enter the new name you wish to give to the style.

   Let's say that it's **Signature**. The Description area lists the characteristics of the selected paragraph.

6. If you want to change these characteristics, click on **Format** and select **Font**.

7. Choose **Bold**, for example, instead of Regular. Click on **OK** to close the Font dialog and return to the New Style dialog box.

8. Confirm your formatting choices in the New Style dialog by clicking on **OK**. This takes you back to the Style dialog.

9. If you wish to create or modify additional styles, proceed with any of the choices listed in step 2. Otherwise, close the Style dialog with one of the following buttons:

   - **Apply**. Applies and saves any changes you have made.

   - **Cancel**. Closes the dialog box without applying your changes.

■ Modifying a style sheet

To improve or modify a style sheet, there is a style repair and restoration workshop. To access this, click on **Format/Style** with the sheet serving as a loaded template. The dialog box that appears allows you to select the styles one by one and adjust their characteristics.

To create several signature styles, for example with an engraved or embossed format, perform the following:

1. Place the cursor on the signature name.
2. Press **Ctrl+Shift+S**.
3. Enter a name (Signature 1).
4. Repeat the operation a few times with Signature 2, 3, 4.

5. Select **Format/Style** in the toolbar. You now access a style collection containing these new styles which you can modify.

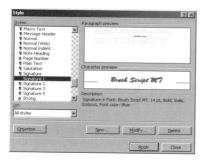

Figure 4.3 Choosing a style for your signature.

To modify one, you need only click on the style of your choice.

Figure 4.4 The Modify Style dialog box.

You will note that some styles are based on others.

Any modification of a basic style will affect any styles based on it. Make your changes. Don't forget to select the **Add to template** and **Automatically update** buttons. When you have finished, press **Apply** to leave the final window. You should now have a variety of signature formats at your disposal.

Figure 4.5 Try different styles before changing any.

 *A style has been modified in a way you did not expect. Check that the **Automatically update** button is activated for the current style. When that is the case, the style is updated whenever you modify it, which ensures consistent styling for the various document elements (for example, the headings). To deactivate this function, select the **Format** menu, click on **Style**, select the style concerned and then click on **Modify**. If the **Automatically update** box is active, deactivate it.*

■ Adopting styles from another document

To adopt the styles contained in another document, perform the following:

1. Open the **Format** menu.
2. Select the **Style** option.
3. Click on the **Organizer** button.
4. Choose the file containing the styles to be copied.
5. Select **Copy**.
6. Rename the **AutoText, Toolbars** and **Macro Project Items** styles.

■ The AutoFormat command

The **AutoFormat** command formats a document using the styles of the template selected in the document style list box.

To choose from other templates, perform the following:

1. Click on the document format you want.
2. Confirm your selection by pressing **OK**.

The predefined document format of your choice is applied to your letter.

 *The **AutoFormat** command lets you customise the look of your document with the help of styles stored in other templates.*

■ Printing styles

To print the style sheet you have just defined, perform the following steps:

1. Select the **File** menu.
2. Click on **Print**.
3. In the **Print what?** box select **Styles**.

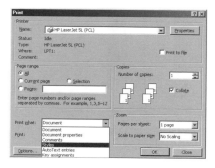

Figure 4.6 Printing styles in the Print dialog box.

■ Choosing a template

With style sheets, you can modify a document format by copying styles.

Another solution is to use a template, enter your text and save it under another name.

What is a template?

A template is a document saved in a predefined format. To apply a standard style sheet to a document, carry out the following steps:

1. Open the **File** menu.
2. Click on **New**.
3. Select the template of your choice.
4. Select the **Create New Document** option.

Figure 4.7 Activating the Create New Document radio button.

In your document, before entering any text, first test the different styles on offer:

1. Open the styles box located at the extreme left of the Formatting toolbar, then type a word or a phrase of your choice.

2. Click on the name of a style. It will automatically be applied to your choice.

You can run through all the standard templates supplied by Microsoft. They are usually located in the **C:\Program Files\Microsoft Office\Templates** subdirectory. They have the file extension .dot. You can access them by clicking on the **File/New** command.

The tabs offer a number of template categories. There are several ways of displaying lists of templates:

- icons;
- list;
- details.

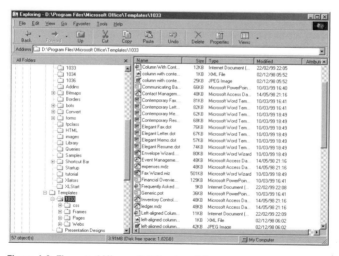

Figure 4.8 The set of Microsoft Office templates.

*The **Templates** and **Add-Ins...** option of the expanding Tools menu attaches another template to the active document, loads Add-Ins or updates the styles in a document. This command*

also loads additional templates in the form of global templates, so that you may use their macros, autotext insertions and customised commands.

■ Creating a template

If you are asked for a precisely formatted document, you can create a suitable style sheet for it. In the example which follows, you can create a template for a personalised letter.

It is made up of standard elements, as follows:

Dear Sir or Madam,

Subject:

My address etc.

My letter

My signature

To create a style sheet, proceed as before:

1. Open the **File** menu.
2. Select **New**.
3. Click on the **General** tab.
4. Choose **Blank Document**.
5. Select the **Create New Document** radio button.

Here is the resulting page once the formatting has been applied. In practice, you will complete the document by inserting the name, address and date on the page.

Once your work is complete, you must save it and give it a name with the .dot extension. To improve this template, we can insert some styles:

1. In documentname.dot, click on an element for which you wish to keep the style.

2. Press **Ctrl+Shift+S**.

3. The text in the style box at the left end of the toolbar will become selected. Enter the name of the style for your selected element.

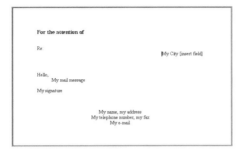

Figure 4.9 Creating your own template!

■ Adding macros

When finished, the page, stored in its folder, is a template available to anyone who uses the computer. It contains elements of presentation, style and text all ready for use: addressee, place and date, signatures and details.

It can still be improved by the addition of macros. You can create, for example, a library of signatures created with WordArt, or again, some personalised headers and footers.

The first step is to become familiar with **WordArt**, so you are aware of what you can achieve. Having once defined your aim, just perform the following steps:

1. Activate the WordArt Toolbar with **View\Toolbars\ WordArt**.

2. Click on **Tools\Macro\Record New Macro**.

3. Enter a short name, for example S1 for 'Signature 2'.

4. Decide where to store the macro (in Normal.dot or only in the open file).

5. Start recording the macro.

6. Click on the **A** button (first set it to blue).

7. Build the signature of your choice (for WordArt, see Chapter 7).

8. Stop recording.

9. Repeat the sequence several times, to obtain a varied choice of original signatures named S1, S2, S3...

Figure 4.10 Creating your first macro.

Templates can be as numerous as you like. They are adaptable to most situations. Enhanced with macros, they provide a whole new environment.

*To learn how to program macros in Visual Basic 6, begin by creating a simple macro. Then click on **Tools/Macro/Macros** and select the one you have just recorded. Select the **Edit** command. The Word 2000 coding for your macro is instantly displayed for your information.*

5 Improving a first draft

■ Finding a word and replacing it with another

Let's imagine that you have used a term wrongly somewhere in your text. Rather than deleting the term ten times and ten times replacing it by another, you can use the **Find** and **Replace** functions. Suppose that in our Bird Watching text, it is necessary to replace all occurrences of 'bird watchers' with the word 'twitchers'.

1. Open the **Edit** menu.
2. Click on the **Replace** option.
3. Select the **Replace** tab.
4. Enter the word to find and replace in the **Find what** text field of the **Find and Replace** dialog box.

Figure 5.1 The Find and Replace dialog box.

5. Enter 'bird watchers' in the **Find what** box and 'twitchers' in the **Replace with** box.
6. Confirm the entry by clicking on the **Replace All** button.

In your text, every occurrence of 'bird watchers' will be replaced by 'twitchers'.

■ Using AutoCorrect

Word 6 launched the concept of autocorrection: Word 2000 perfects it. The **AutoCorrect** function on the **Tools** menu permits the user to make corrections while typing.

Let's say that you have written a long report where the name International Court for Human Rights appears at least ten times. Also, you have the tendency to invert certain letters and type 'puls' for 'plus'. Before entering your report, prepare the ground:

1. Open a document that you name, for example, Error 01, and write the two terms that concern you:

   ■ International Court for Human Rights;

   ■ plus.

2. Begin by selecting 'International Court for Human Rights'.

3. Open the **Tools** menu.

4. Click on **AutoCorrect**.

In the right column are the substitute words and in the left column the terms before substitution.

Figure 5.2 **Corrections while you type**.

5. 'International Court for Human Rights' is entered in the column on the right, and you type 'ICHR' in the left-hand column.

When you go on to key in your text, each time you type 'ICHR' the full name will appear in the text. Talk about saving time! Repeat this same operation with 'plus' and all the other words that you tend to mis-spell.

Complete a word automatically

The AutoComplete function automatically saves time when entering certain words. It can add the last letters of the days of the week, of months, and the last digits of the day's date.

> October
> The·month·of·octo|

Figure 5.3 The word October is completed automatically.

Let's take the example of Saturday, which is composed of eight letters. When you have typed the fourth letter, the word Saturday appears automatically in a ScreenTip. Press **Enter** to confirm it and the word Saturday is completed for you. Counting the validation stroke, you have saved three key strokes: rather than type r, d, a, y, you just press Enter.

■ Finding doubles

Besides suggesting corrections for incorrectly spelled words, the spell checker also corrects doubles; that is, terms repeated twice in a row. You are even presented with a thorough explanation, as you can see in Figure 5.4.

 *The **Next Sentence** box selects the next sentence in the active document to be checked for spelling and grammar.*

 *Remember that you can set the Spellchecker to check for different languages, from **Tools**, **Language**, **Set Language**. Once you have selected your language, click on **Default**, **Yes**, **OK** to apply.*

Figure 5.4 The Spellchecker has identified a double occurrence in your text.

*If you are consistently using a foreign word, such as Muscadet, for example, Word 2000 will offer to replace it with a number of what may well appear as ridiculous suggestions (in this case, Muscatel, Muscoda, Miscode, Mustarded and so on). Ignore suggestions by clicking on **Ignore** or **Ignore All**.*

■ Finding synonyms

Word 2000 puts a thesaurus of synonyms at your disposal.

1. Select the word for which you would like a synonym; for example, 'lovely'.
2. Open the **Tools** menu.
3. Select the **Language** option.
4. Select **Thesaurus**. A dialog box opens which offers you synonyms for the word 'lovely' based on a standard dictionary entry. In addition you are offered the meanings of the word 'lovely'. Select the word which you want to replace 'lovely'.
5. Click on the **Replace** button.

Equally you have the chance to make a search on a word of your choice. The thesaurus will offer you synonyms and definitions for it.

Let's suppose you would like a synonym for 'excursion'.

1. Select **Tools/Language/Thesaurus**.
2. Enter 'excursion' in the text box.
3. Click on **Look Up** and the thesaurus will offer you multiple synonyms.

Figure 5.5 The synonyms of 'excursion'.

■ Creating your own dictionary

The spelling checker compares the terms in your text to those in its dictionary (with thousands of standard words). It is probable that certain words and expressions that you use may not figure in this lexicon, notably any technical terms related to your profession. You can create personal dictionaries which the spelling checker will consult for each correction.

This is how it's done:

1. Open the **Tools** menu.
2. Choose **Options**.
3. Click on the **Spelling and Grammar** tab.
4. Click on the **Dictionaries...** button.

Figure 5.6 The Custom Dictionaries dialog box.

5. Press the **New** button in the **Custom Dictionaries** dialog box.

In the filename zone, enter a name for your dictionary, for example 'MyDictionary'.

The access path for your new dictionary will be:

C:\Program Files\Common Files\Microsoft Shared\Proof\ MyDictionary.dic

■ Using AutoText

The **Insert** menu lists elements for insertion into your documents, such as private or professional letters. Click in a document location where you would like to make an AutoText insertion.

Using the Insert menu

1. Open the **Insert** menu.
2. Select the **AutoText** submenu.

The submenu lists a choice of items to insert; for example, standard greetings or closures, mailing instructions and so on.

Figure 5.7 Various possible automatic insertions.

3. Click on an expression suitable for your letter: it will be inserted automatically. The expressions for insertion can be modified at any time.

Using the Insert toolbar.

The **AutoText** button on your **AutoText** toolbar (available from the **View** menu) allows you to list, insert, modify or delete items for insertion.

■ Extracting document statistics

This function is very useful if you work with people who evaluate documents by the number of characters contained within them. This is the case for most editors of magazines, periodicals, reviews and so on.

Figure 5.8 Extracting document statistics.

A page holds 1500 characters. When you enter your text, you can check the number of characters at any time, as follows:

1. Select the text.
2. Open the **File** menu.
3. Select the **Properties** option.
4. Activate the **Statistics** tab.

Bird Watching has 1 page, 3 paragraphs, 7 lines, 52 words, 242 characters, 291 characters (with spaces).

*The **Word Count...** option on the **Tools** menu counts the number of pages, words, characters, paragraphs and lines contained in the active document. Punctuation marks and special characters are included in the count.*

■ Requesting an AutoSummary

Word 2000 performs statistical and linguistic analyses of documents. It determines which are the most important

■■■

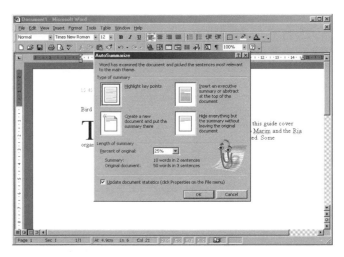

Figure 5.9 Automatic summary.

phrases. The **AutoSummarize** function allows the user to see
quickly what is in a document. The key points of the text are
listed.

To read the summary of a document on line, the document
must be screened in automatic summary mode. The screen
mode offers two options: display only the key points of the text
or display the whole document with key points highlighted.

Let's put Bird Watching to the AutoSummary test:

1. Open the **Tools** menu.

2. Click on **AutoSummarize...** the AutoSummarize dialog
   box appears.

3. Select **Hide everything but the summary without leaving the
   original document**. From our text of 242 characters, the
   summary, 25 per cent of the text, has retained a key pas-
   sage where it says that 'Some organisations arrange bird
   watching trips'.

Figure 5.10 Bird Watching puts AutoSummarize to the test.

You can control the size of summary that you want displayed.

■ Calling up the Office Assistant

As soon as you start to write the salutation of a letter, 'Dear', for example, followed by the name of the person you are writing to, the Office Assistant asks you if you need help to compose your document.

1. Write 'Dear friend'.

Figure 5.11 The Office Assistant.

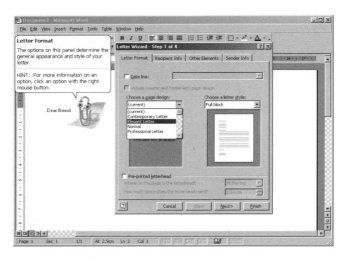

Figure 5.12 Letter Wizard – composing a letter with elegant page design.

2. Press Enter. The Office Assistant appears and asks you:

- if would you like help with writing the letter; or
- if you want to type the letter without help.

3. Click on the **Get help with writing the letter** button.

The Office Assistant offers you a series of parameters for you to specify (sender, recipient, letter style (letter format – contemporary, normal, professional, elegant). It's your choice.

If you haven't installed the Office Assistant, you can request it as follows:

1. Open the **File** menu.

2. Click on **New**.

3. Select the **Letters and Faxes** tab.

4. Double-click a **Wizard**.

■ Inserting comments

You may insert comments relating to your text.

1. Open the **Insert** menu.
2. Click on the **Comment** option.
3. Select the word or group of words where you wish to add a comment.

   For example, if you select the word 'excursion' it will be highlighted in yellow.
4. In the text input zone at the bottom of the screen, enter the comment that you wish to attach to the word.

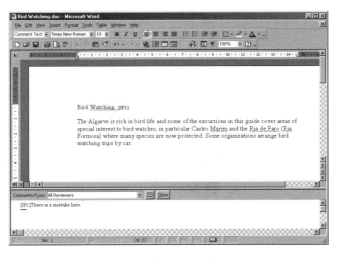

Figure 5.13 Enter a comment at the bottom of the screen.

■ Tracking changes

Word 2000 allows you to check the sequence of changes to a document. To track changes, proceed as follows:

1. Open the **Tools** menu.
2. Select the **Track Changes** option.
3. Choose **Highlight changes on screen**: the changes to your document will appear on your screen.
4. Click on **Options** to customise the way in which the changes will appear on your screen.

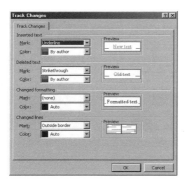

Figure 5.14 Choose how changes will appear on the screen.

Displaying today's changes

You can refine your specification, if you want to display changes made in such and such a period.

1. Open the **Tools** menu.
2. Select **Track Changes/Compare Documents**.
3. Open the **Last modified** list.
4. Select **today**. You have the choice between:
   - today;
   - any time;
   - this week;
   - last week;

- this month;
- last month.

5. Click on the **Find Now** button. The text area lists the files modified today.

6. Click on the **Open** command button. The files modified today will open.

 Displaying changes consists of highlighting the changes made to the content of a file, including moved or pasted text, inserted or deleted lines and columns.

6 Working with columns

Presenting a document in columns
Creating a heading across several columns
Inserting a picture
Changing the number of columns
Adding separating lines
Setting the spacing between columns
Setting column widths
Previewing columns
Column length
Removing columns
Calling up the Newsletter Wizard

■ Presenting a document in columns

The **Columns** view allows text to be displayed in several columns (up to 12) within a single section. There is a correlation between the legibility of a text and the number of columns. Text in columns is easier to read than text in a single block: the daily newspapers use this type of presentation quite intentionally.

Word 2000 allows you to change the layout of your document into columns. On one page, it is possible to present some text in two columns and other text in three columns.

You decide to present Bird Watching in a magazine page format composed of two columns. Here's how it's done:

1. Firstly type in the whole of your text.
2. Place the cursor below the title.
3. Open the **Insert** menu.
4. Select the **Break** option.
5. Select the **Continuous** radio button in the **Section** area (you don't want a page break) in the **Break** dialog box.

Figure 6.1 The Break dialog box.

6. Place the cursor in the second section of your text.
7. Open the **Format** menu.
8. Select the **Columns...** option.

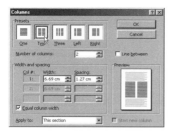

Figure 6.2 In the Columns dialog box, select the Two box.

9. Click on **Two**.

   Go into **Page Layout** view if necessary.

10.   Place the cursor at the end of the first column.

11.   Select **Insert/Break/Column** break.

Your document is now set in two columns. You can now go ahead and format it using justification and so on.

Bird Watching .

The Algarve is rich in bird life and some of the excursions in this guide cover areas of special interest to bird watches, in particular Castro Marim and the Ria de Faro (Ria Formosa) where many species are now protected. Some organizations arrange bird watching trips by car.

Boat Services.

There is a boat service from Vila Real to Ayamonte in Spain. It operates 24 hours a day from 1 June to 30 September and also at Christmas. The rest of the year it runs from 0700 to 2300 (0800 to midnight Spanish time). There are boats from Faro out to its beaches, from Olhao to the islands of Culatra and Armona, from the Tavira to Ilha de Tavira.

Figure 6.3 Your text is now set in two columns.

Word calculates the number of columns you can create on the one page as a function of four parameters: page width, margin width, column width and spacing.

■ Creating a heading across several columns

This is how to create a heading across several columns:

1. If your text is not yet set in columns, create the columns.
2. In **Page Layout** view, select the text for the heading.
3. Click on **Columns** and then select **One column** in the **Columns** dialog box.

■ Inserting a picture

To insert a picture in one of your columns, you must first insert a frame. How is this done?

1. Open the **Insert** menu.
2. Select the **Picture** option.

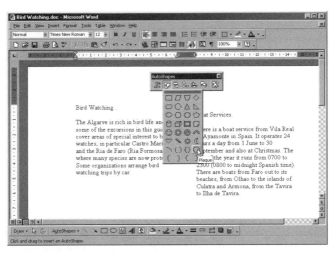

Figure 6.4 Insert the Rounded Rectangle shape.

3. Click on **AutoShapes**.

4. Select the shape which suits you best, for example **Rounded Rectangle**.

5. Click. Your cursor changes to a cross.

6. Place the cursor where you want to insert the Rounded Rectangle.

7. Open the **Insert** menu.

8. Select the **Text Box** option.

9. Choose a picture from your .bmp image files and display it in **Paint**.

10. Open the **Paint Edit** menu.

11. Click on **Copy**. Your picture is in the Clipboard.

12. Return to your Bird Watching document.

13. Place your cursor in the 'Rounded Rectangle Frame'.

14. Open the **Edit** menu.

15. Select **Paste**.

Your picture now appears in the text.

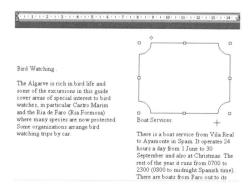

Figure 6.5 Your cursor changes into a cross. Place it where you want to insert your Rounded Rectangle.

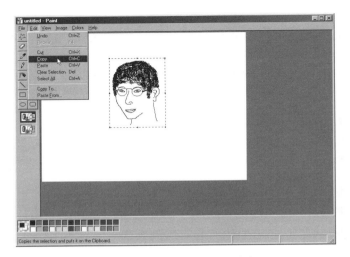

Figure 6.6 Using the Paint utility, copy your desired picture
to the clipboard.

Paint (previously called **PaintBrush**) is a simple utility for
creating pictures. Amongst other things, it allows you to retrieve
an image obtained by using the Print Screen key or the
Alt+Print Scrn keyboard shorcut, and then to edit it.

■ Changing the number of columns

To change the number of columns in your document, perform the following:

1. Change to **Print Layout** view.
2. Select the whole document.
3. Open the **Edit** menu.

Figure 6.7 If you installed the Columns utility, it allows you
to select the desired number of columns.

4. Click on **Select All**.

5. Open the **Format** menu.

6. Click on the **Columns** option.

7. Select **Three**.

 To change the number of columns in a document, select the ***Edit*** *menu and* ***Redo columns***. *Your text will return to the number of columns that it had originally.*

■ Adding separating lines

To add separating lines between your columns, change to
Print Layout view. If your document is split into sections,
perform the following:

1. Click in the section to be modified.

2. Open the **Format** menu.

3. Select the **Columns** option.

4. Tick the **Line between** check box.

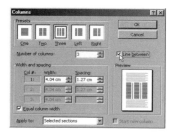

Figure 6.8 The Line between check box in the Columns dialog box.

■ Setting the spacing between columns

You can change the spacing between columns at any time. By default, the spacing is 1.27 cm. If you want to create multiple columns, reduce this spacing. You can also increase it. Two methods are available for setting the spacing between columns: with the Columns dialog box or by using the ruler.

By using the ruler

1. Open the **View** menu.
2. Activate the **Ruler** option. The grey areas of the ruler represent the spacing between the columns.
3. Place your cursor on one of the grey margin limits. It changes into a double-headed arrow.
4. Press and drag the arrow cursors on the ruler to increase or reduce the spacing between the columns. You can move them left or right. If **Equal column width** is activated for a document, changes will apply to both columns.

With the Columns dialog box

To change the spacing between columns using the dialog box, perform the following:

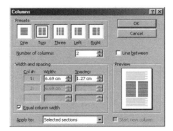

Figure 6.9 The Width and Spacing section of the dialog box allows you to set the spacing between columns.

1. Place the insertion point in the section you wish to change.
2. Open the **Format** menu.
3. Select the **Columns** option. The dialog box is displayed.
4. Use the **Width** and **Spacing** adjustment arrows in the **Width and spacing** section of the dialog box.

■ Setting column widths

To set column widths, the path to follow is essentially the same as for setting the column spacing.

You can change it by dragging the margin markers on the ruler, or with the aid of the dialog box. Columns may have different widths. It is possible to spread text evenly across columns.

Using the ruler

1. Open the **View** menu.
2. Activate the **Ruler** option.
3. Slide the cursor along the ruler. It changes into a double-headed arrow.

4. With the mouse button depressed, slide the column markers to increase or reduce the column widths.

Via the Columns dialog box

1. Open the **Format** menu.
2. Select **Columns** to open the **Columns** dialog box.
3. In the **Width and Spacing** section, use the **Width** adjustment arrows to set the column widths.

If the text in the columns is wider than foreseen, you have almost certainly applied a negative indent to the first line of the text. Click in the text, then check the ruler. If an indent marker is located to the right or left of the column marker, slide it into alignment with the column marker.

■ Previewing columns

If you have not yet managed to view the newspaper-style columns you have just created, there are two possible explanations: your text is not long enough to need two columns or you are in Normal view.

To display the limits of newspaper-type columns, here are various steps to take:

1. Change to **Print Layout** view.
2. Open the **Tools** menu.
3. Click on **Options**.
4. Activate the **View** tab.
5. In the **Show** section, tick the **Text boundaries** check box.

The boundaries of the text are displayed on the screen.

Figure 6.10 Tick the Text boundaries box on the View tab of the Options dialog.

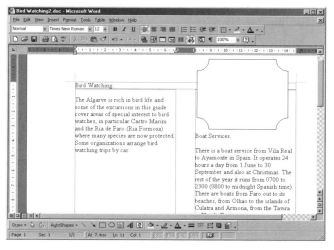

Figure 6.11 The text boundaries are displayed on the screen.

To display hidden text, tick the **Hidden text** box on the **View** tab.

■ Column length

If your text is long, organised in several columns and many pages long, it is important that the columns have the same length and width throughout. Word 2000 evens up the length of the columns and aligns them automatically. However, your text may still contain a widowed or orphaned column. On one page, for example, there can be three full columns and one half-full, because your text ends there. Here's how to remedy this:

1. Place the insertion point at the end of the text.
2. Open the **Insert** menu.
3. Select the **Break** option.
4. Tick the **Continuous** radio button in the **Section break** area.
5. Confirm it by pressing the **OK** button.

Figure 6.12 The Compatibility tab of the Options dialog box.

Your columns will be balanced by the insertion of a section break at the end of the document.

 *Do not forget to deactivate the **Don't balance columns for Continuous section starts** check box! You will find this box in the Options area of the **Compatibility** tab of the **Tools/Options** dialog box.*

■ Removing columns

You can remove any columns in your document with the help of the Columns option dialog box:

1. Place the insertion point in the document section you wish to alter.
2. Open the **Format** menu.
3. Select the **Columns** option.
4. Click on **One** in the **Presets** group.

■ Calling up the Newsletter Wizard

The Newsletter Wizard produces a newsletter according to your instructions. How do you get this help?

1. Open the **File** menu.
2. Click on **New**.
3. Click the **Publications** tab.
4. Select the Newsletter Wizard, install it or select Calendar, Brochure, Manual etc. according to your need.

   A newsletter is created on the basis of three criteria:

   ■ **Style & Color.** The style can be professional, contemporary or elegant.

Figure 6.13 The Newsletter Wizard asks which style to use for your letter.

- **Title & Content.** Detail the title and (optionally) the date and volume number.
- **Mailing Label.** It's possible to reserve a space on the back of the letter for a mailing label.

5. Go on to the next Newsletter Wizard dialog box by clicking on the **Next** button.

6. Click on the **Finish** button when your template is complete.

7. If you click on the Office Assistant icon, the Office Assistant appears and offers you two types of assistance:

- help with the Newsletter Wizard;
- help in general.

Regarding Style & Color, the Office Assistant informs you that the example newsletter text provides additional information on adding components to and formatting the newsletter.

7 Illustrating a document

■ Customising the Drawing toolbar

Word 2000 offers more numerous and more powerful drawing tools than Word 97 (which was already innovative in this
field) and, comparing them with other currently available
utilities, one realises to what extent Microsoft has built into
Word tools previously reserved for specialised graphic illustration software. In many instances, there is no need to quit
Word 2000: you can customise the Drawing toolbar instead.

These very useful tools include:

- **Edit Wrap Points.** Lets you run text around part of an
  image, for example to wrap round a sphere so that the
  closest letters are all the same distance from the circum-
  ference.

- **Set Transparent Color.** Sets the colour you wish to make
  transparent. You can use transparent areas to integrate a
  picture on your page – for example, when you have a picture of a person and don't want the background colour to
  be visible.

- **Crop.** Allows you to reframe a picture.

- **More/Less Brightness/Contrast.** Four tools to adjust the
  colours. Over- or under-exposed photos are now quickly
  corrected.

- **Depth.** Adjusts the depth of 3-D objects.

- **Shadow Settings.** A set of tools to switch the shadow
  effect on and off, attribute a colour to the shadow, and
  move the shadow stepwise up/down/left/right (nudge).

- **Rotate or Flip.** A set of tools for rotating and flipping
  objects.

Once loaded, the Drawing toolbar, relatively modest to start
with, can offer an impressive array of tools.

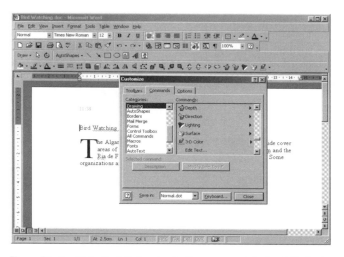

Figure 7.1 To obtain the full Drawing toolbar, you must first add the tools with the Customize command in the View/Toolbar menu – as described in Chapter 1.

■ Creating a title in 3-D

In Word 2000 WordArt, you can add a 3-D effect to lines, shapes and objects with the 3-D tool on the Drawing toolbar. 3-D options allow you to change the depth of a drawing as well as its colour, angle, illumination direction and surface reflection. To change a drawing's 3-D effect, click on **3-D Settings** (3-D submenu) and then use the 3-D Settings toolbar.

The five effects buttons on the **3-D Settings** toolbar allow you to specify parameters for:

- Depth;
- Direction;

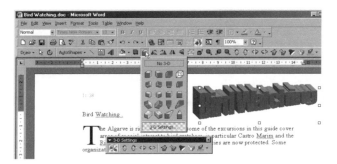

Figure 7.2 3-D Settings.

- Lighting;
- Surface;
- 3-D Color (Automatic).

For example, to change a lighting effect do the following:

1. Select your title 'Bird Watching'.
2. Click on the **3-D** button, then on **3-D Settings**.
3. In the 3-D Settings toolbar, click on **Lighting**, then select the **Dim** option.
4. Click on the **Depth** button and set the depth in points for your title, for example 72 or 144 points.

■ Inserting a WordArt object

You can create titles and texts in 3-D thanks to the WordArt utility:

1. Open the **Insert** menu.
2. Open the **Picture** submenu.
3. Click on **WordArt**.

Figure 7.3 The Insert WordArt button on the Drawing toolbar.

You can also use the WordArt button on the Drawing toolbar, which gives you access to 30 shapes with predefined effects.

How do you create a title with WordArt predefined styles?

1. Select your title 'Bird Watching'.

2. Delete it.

3. Place the insertion point where you wish to insert your new title with special WordArt styling.

4. Click on the **Insert WordArt** button (Drawing toolbar).

5. Double-click the WordArt style of your choice.

6. Enter your title in the **Edit WordArt Text** dialog box.

7. Select font and point size.

8. Click on **OK**. Your title is then displayed showing the chosen effect.

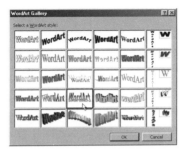

Figure 7.4: Predefined WordArt effects.

Now you can either leave your title as is or apply additional modifications, for example, perform a free rotation on it:

1. Select the title and click on the **Free Rotate** button. The cursor changes into a white arrow with a circular arrow at its point, indicating a rotation direction.

2. Drag this handle to rotate the title.

Figure 7.5 The rotate handles appear in green, with a circular black arrow.

Figure 7.6 Before the rotate movement.

Figure 7.7 After the rotate movement.

The **WordArt Shape** option, indicated by the **Abc** icon, allows you to change this title even further, to show one of 40 different new looks, including:

- Stop;
- Triangle Up/Down;
- Chevron Up/Down;
- Arch Up/Down (Curve/Pour);
- Button (Curve/Pour);
- Inflate (Bottom/Top);
- Deflate (Bottom/Top);
- Fade Right/Left/Up/Down.

To apply a WordArt shape, do the following:

1. Click on your **3-D** title to activate it.
2. Click on **Abc**.
3. Select a shape, for example **Ring Inside**.

Figure 7.8 The Ring Inside and other WordArt shapes.

Figure 7.9 WordArt shapes let you distort your titles in many ways.

Your title now has the predefined style, plus the Ring Inside shape.

■ Editing text

The **Edit Text** button on the WordArt toolbar allows you to edit your text at any time, without changing its predefined style.

1. Select the WordArt object.
2. Click on the **Edit Text** button on the WordArt toolbar. The **Edit Text** dialog box appears on the screen. You can change the font, point size and character style and make all kinds of other changes to your text.

Resizing a WordArt object

Once it has been inserted in your document, you can change the size of your WordArt object so that it takes up the whole page or measures only a few centimetres.

■ Changing colour

With the **Fill Color** button on the Drawing toolbar, you can change the colours of predefined WordArt objects at any time.

1. Click on the **WordArt object** inserted in your text.

2. Using the **Fill Color** drop-down arrow, open the colour palette of the Fill Color button, which adds a colour or a fill effect to the selected object. It can also modify or remove an effect or a colour. The fill effects are grouped under **Gradient, Texture, Pattern** and **Picture**.

■ The spacing of a WordArt object

To set the spacing of a WordArt object, click on the **AV** button on the WordArt toolbar to open the character spacing menu.

You can set the text characters in your object to be **Very Tight, Tight, Normal, Loose, Very Loose,** or opt for **Custom**.

Custom spacing
Custom spacing automatically adjusts the spacing for certain letter combinations to give a word a more evenly spaced look. This setting only works with True Type fonts or Adobe Type Manager.

■ WordArt object parameters

To set the parameters for a WordArt object, click on the **Format WordArt** button on the WordArt toolbar, which opens a dialog box where you can work on **Colors and Lines, Size, Layout, Wrapping, Fill** and so on.

■ Lighting a 3–D object

To create another title in 3-D and set the lighting, perform the following:

Figure 7.10 Enter your text in the Edit WordArt Text dialog box.

1. Select the **Insert WordArt** button.
2. Double-click a predefined 3-D style.
3. Type Bird Watching in the **Edit WordArt Text** dialog box's Text area.
4. Press the **OK** button.
5. Select the object.

Click on the **Lighting** icon on the 3-D Settings toolbar. You can set the intensity and direction of the lighting. Start with the intensity.

There are three options:

- Bright;
- Normal;
- Dim.

6. Click on **Bright**.

Figure 7.11 The Bright option in the 3-D Settings Lighting dialog.

Figure 7.12 Your 3-D title with modified lighting.

Now set the lighting direction.

There are nine possible options, including:

- left side;
- right side;
- from below;
- from above;
- central.

Central lighting gives your object the most striking intensity.

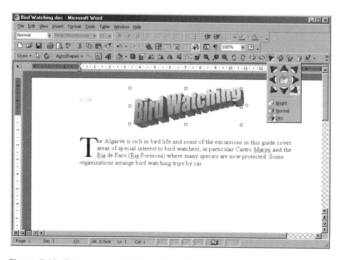

Figure 7.13 Set your own lighting direction.

■ Adding a shadow

You can add a shadow to a shape or a drawing using the **Shadow** button on the Drawing toolbar.

To adjust the position of the shadow or to change its colour:

1. Click on the **Shadow Settings** option of the Drawing toolbar Shadow button.

You can add a shadow or a 3-D effect, but not both at the same time. If you apply a 3-D style to a design that already has a shadow, the shadow disappears.

■ Inserting AutoShapes

You can enhance your text at any time by adding an AutoShape from among the hundred or so offered by Word 2000:

1. Click the **AutoShapes** button on the Drawing toolbar, or open the **Insert** menu.
2. Select the **Picture/AutoShapes** option. Six categories of AutoShapes are offered:
   - **Lines;**
   - **Basic Shapes;**
   - **Block Arrows;**
   - **Flowchart;**
   - **Stars and Banners;**
   - **Callouts.**
3. Select **Callouts**.
4. Select **Cloud Callout**.
5. Position this shape at a suitable place in the text.

Figure 7.14 The Cloud Callout shape in the Callouts option.

6. Click on the **Text Box** icon in the Drawing toolbar. The cursor changes to a cross: move it to the inside of the Cloud Callout.

7. Write a comment of your choice inside the callout.

 Comic strip cartoons have successfully instituted the term **Callout** *as a word in common usage for the callout's shape.*

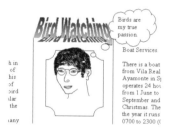

Figure 7.15 Your different formatting effect illustrations brought together.

■ Putting a drawing in front of or behind text

You can choose one of three levels in which to insert a drawing or AutoShape:

- in the same layer as the text;
- behind the text;
- in front of the text.

At the moment of insertion, a drawing is always in front of the text, floating on it. If you want to put it behind the text, perform the following steps:

1. Open the **Draw** menu on the Drawing toolbar.
2. Select **Order**.
3. Click on **Send Behind Text**.

■ Running text around irregular objects

To run text around irregular objects, execute the following steps:

1. Open the **View** menu.
2. Open the **Toolbars** submenu.
3. Click on the **Customize** option.
4. Select **Toolbar/Picture**. The Picture Toolbar appears.
5. Select the **Text Box** icon.
6. Once the text box is open, right-click it.
7. Select the **Text Wrapping** option.
8. Different styles of wrapping are displayed.
9. Select **Top** and **Bottom**.

Figure 7.16 Top and Bottom wrapping for an irregular object.

Figure 7.17 Writing around irregular objects.

10. Enter your text.

11. Crop your picture.

12. Paste it inside the text box.

The text immediately divides around the irregular object, above and below.

■ Customising a page border

Word 2000 allows you to surround each page with a customised border. Apart from 150 new line and border styles, Word 2000 contains just as many artistic border styles stemming from the BorderArt utility, part of Microsoft Publisher.

To access these:

1. Open the **Format** menu.

2. Select the **Borders and Shading** submenu or click on the **Border** icon of the **Tables and Borders** toolbar.

- To place a border around a paragraph, click anywhere in the paragraph.

- To place a border around a specific text or a certain word, select it.

- To enclose only specific edges, click in the Preview section on the side or sides you want.

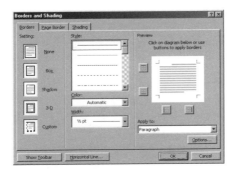

Figure 7.18 **Creating a customised border.**

To specify the exact position of the border in relation to the text:

1. Click on the **Options** button.

2. Select the desired options.

To frame the two pages of your Bird Watching text and customise the frame:

1. Select the **Page Border** tab.

2. Specify the border of your choice.

Figure 7.19 **Preview gives you an idea of the end result.**

8 Creating tables

■ Deciding which Office application to use for your table

You will often have occasion to use tables when word processing. There are several ways of doing this. The first is to use Excel and insert your table into Word via the Clipboard. We recommend this method if you foresee inserting complex calculations, statistical analyses or diagrams in your table. If you need to use sophisticated techniques or relational data base type search or filter commands, it would be much better to use Microsoft Access.

Word 2000 is particularly effective for creating tables containing complex graphic formatting: bulleted lists, customised tabs, numbered lists, first line indents, different formatting cell by cell, or cells split diagonally.

■ Creating a table

Word 2000 facilitates the creation of tables composed of rows and columns defined by yourself. The intersection of a row and a column is called a cell. Inside a cell, you can enter a number, a word, a phrase, a paragraph, a chart or a picture. Each cell is independent. You can insert your table anywhere in the document and resize it if need be, automatically adding a title, a caption, an equation or customised borders.

To insert a table into your document, perform the following steps:

1. Click on the **Insert Table** icon of the **Standard** toolbar.

2. A schematic table composed of five columns and four rows appears. To change these default parameters to your requirements, begin by placing the mouse pointer in the last cell on the bottom right. There, keeping the left mouse

Figure 8.1 Place the cursor on the Insert Table icon of the Standard toolbar.

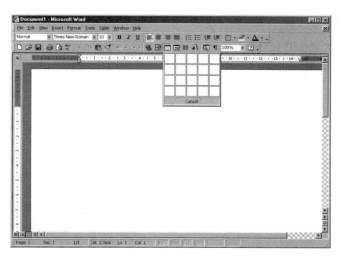

Figure 8.2 Click on the icon to insert a table and design it yourself.

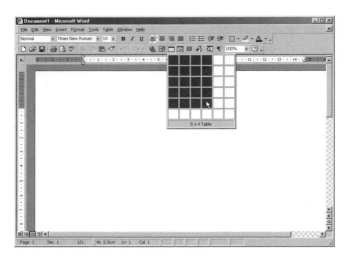

Figure 8.3 Selecting the required number of rows and columns.

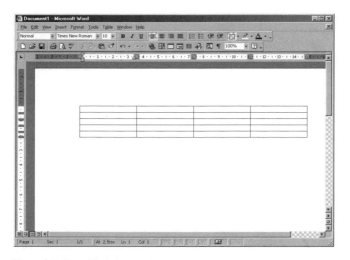

Figure 8.4 The table is inserted into your page.

button depressed, drag the table diagonally to increase or decrease the numbers of columns and rows at will. You are going to need a table with five rows and four columns. When you have selected five rows, drag the cursor across to reduce the selected columns to four. Release the mouse button. The desired table appears in your document. All the columns are the same width.

Now you need to fill the table with information, for example, by entering some text. The insertion point, in the form of a blinking vertical black bar, is located at the beginning of the first cell (that is, column one of row one). To enter your text, perform the following steps:

1. Enter your text in the first cell. In our example, type 'buy'. To move to the next column, use the right-arrow key or the Tab key.

2. In the second column type 'buys', then 'bought' in the third and 'bought' in the fourth. Now move to the next row by pressing the Tab key.

3. Finish filling in your table.

Selecting a cell

To select a cell, click on the cell selection area between the left border of the cell and the beginning of the cell text. When the cursor is over this area, it changes into a black arrow pointing towards top right.

A cell is selected when its background is black, with the text reversed out in white.

buy	buys	bought	bought
lie	lies	lay	lain
cry	cries	cried	cried
lay	lays	laid	laid
see	sees	saw	seen

Figure 8.5 A selected cell in your table appears in reverse; that is, with white letters on a black background.

Changing the size of a cell

To change the height of a cell:

1. Select the text within the cell, including the cell end marker.
2. Using the cursor transformed into two small black arrows pointing up and down, draw the cell out in height.

To change the width of a cell:

1. Select the text within the cell, including the cell end marker.
2. Using the cursor which has changed into two small black arrows pointing left and right, draw the cell out widthways.

Figure 8.6 Using the cell boundary to change the cell width.

Selecting a row

Double-click on the cell selection area. Alternatively, you can use the **Table** menu **Select Row** command.

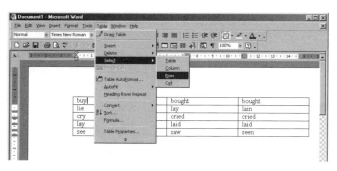

Figure 8.7 Selecting a row.

Selecting a column

To select a column:

1. Place the cursor at the top of the first cell in the column, so that it becomes a black arrow pointing downwards.
2. Click.

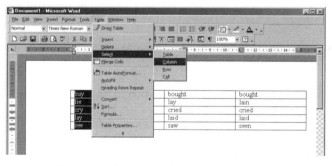

Figure 8.8 Selecting a column.

Alternatively, you can use the **Select Column** option on the **Table** menu.

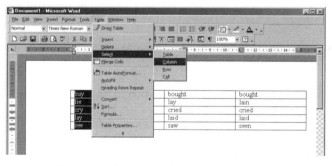

Figure 8.9 Selecting a column using the Table menu.

Selecting a whole table

To select the whole of a table, perform the following:

1. Click in the last cell, at bottom right.
2. Keep the mouse button depressed.
3. Drag the cursor up towards the first cell in the table.

Alternatively you can use the **Select Table** command on the **Table** menu.

■ Modifying the size of a table

As a table evolves, it will have to be be enlarged or reduced as needed. The frequency of these manipulations requires an easy method.

Inserting rows

To insert a row:

1. Select the row above which you want to insert a new row. The **Insert Table** button in the **Standard** toolbar will change name and appearance and become the **Insert Rows** button.

2. Click on the **Insert Rows** button. The newly inserted row is automatically selected; so you can add further rows by simply clicking on the **Insert Rows** button again.

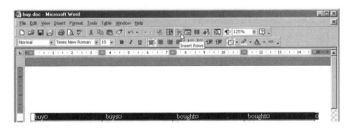

Figure 8.10 Adding a row with the Insert Rows button.

Alternatively, you can use the **Table** menu to insert new rows. Perform the following steps:

1. Place the insertion point in the any cell of the row above or below which you want to insert a new row.

2. Open the **Table** menu and select the **Insert** option.

3. In the submenu that appears, click on **Rows Above** or **Rows Below**.

Figure 8.11 Adding a row with the Table menu.

Inserting columns

To insert a column:

1. Select the column to le left of which you want to insert a new column. The **Insert Table** button in the **Standard** toolbar changes into the **Insert Columns** button.

2. Click on the **Insert Columns** button.

Deleting rows

To delete one or more rows:

1. Select the row or rows that you want to delete.
2. Place your cursor inside the highlighted area.
3. Right-click; the **Table** context menu pops up on your screen.

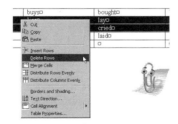

Figure 8.12 Deleting rows with the Table context menu.

4. Select the **Delete Rows** option. The selected row(s) will be deleted immediately, without request for confirmation.

Alternatively, you can delete rows with the **Table** menu:

1. Select the row or rows you want to delete.
2. Open the **Table** menu and select the **Delete** option.
3. In the submenu that appears, select **Rows**. The selected row(s) will be deleted immediately, without request for confirmation.

Figure 8.13 You can delete rows with the Table menu.

Deleting columns

To delete one or more columns:

1. Select the column or columns you wish to delete.
2. Place your cursor inside the highlighted area.
3. Right-click; the **Table** context menu pops up on your screen.
4. Select the **Delete Columns** option.

Alternatively, you can delete columns with the **Table** menu:

1. Select the column or columns you want to delete.
2. Open the **Table** menu and select the **Delete** option.
3. In the submenu that appears, select **Columns**.

Moving rows

To move a row:

1. Select the row.
2. Place the cursor on the selected row.
3. Keeping the mouse button pressed, drag the cursor to the desired new location.

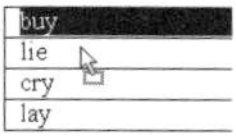

Figure 8.14 Moving a row using drag-and-drop.

Moving columns

To move a column:

1. Select the column.
2. Place the cursor in the selected column.
3. Keeping the mouse button pressed, drag the cursor to the desired new location.

■ Enhancing the appearance of a table

Once the table has been defined, its ease of use can be enhanced. This step is important to improve a user's productivity.

Tabulations

How do you define tab stops with leaders inside your table? Select the column in which you want to integrate leaders before a tabulation.

In our example, this shall concern column one from the first to the fifth row.

1. Open the **Format** menu.
2. Click on **Tabs**.
3. In the Tabs dialog box, enter 2cm as the Tab stop position.
4. Tick the box corresponding to the alignment to be applied to the text; in our case, opt for **Right**.
5. Tick the box corresponding to the desired leader in the Leader area.
6. Click **OK** to confirm your choices and close the dialog.
7. Back in your table, press **Ctrl+Tab**: the leader line appears in your first column.

Figure 8.15 The Tabs dialog box with the Leader option.

buy -----------	buys
lie ------------	lies
cry------------	cries
lay------------	lays
see------------	sees

Figure 8.16 Your table with leader lines.

In the end it's up to you to make the enhancements and changes you think fit, such as:

■ title centre alignment;
■ colour rectification;
■ deleting leaders.

INFINITIVE	THIRD PERSON	PAST TENSE	PAST PARTICIPLE
buy	buys	bought	bought
lie	lies	lay	lain
cry	cries	cried	cried
lay	lays	laid	laid
see	sees	saw	seen

Figure 8.17 Your formatted table.

Distributing columns and rows evenly

To distribute the columns evenly:

1. Select several columns
2. Open the **Table** menu.
3. Click on **Distribute Columns Evenly.**

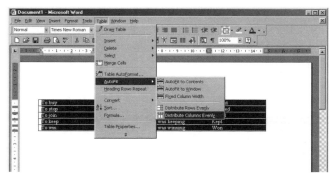

Figure 8.18 Evenly distribute the columns in your table.

To distribute the rows evenly:

1. Select several rows.
2. Open the **Table** menu.
3. Click on **Distribute Rows Evenly.**

Merging cells

To insert a title row that spreads over the full width of your table, you need to perform two actions: first insert a row and then merge its cells. To insert the title row:

1. Place the insertion point in the row, above the cell where you want to insert a title row.
2. Open the **Table** menu.
3. Click on the **Insert Rows** option.

With this you obtain a row split into four parts, corresponding to your four columns. To merge these cells into one and insert the title:

1. Select all the cells to be merged (here the entire first row).
2. Select the **Merge Cells** option.
3. Place the insertion point in the new non-split row.
4. Enter a title.
5. Enhance your text.
6. Centre it by clicking on the **Centre** icon.

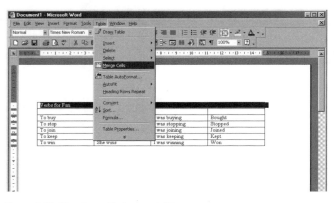

Figure 8.19 Merging cells in your table.

In Word, merging cells means to reassemble in a single cell the contents of several consecutive cells. In Excel, merging cells means to reassemble in a single cell the contents of two or more selected cells. The reference of a merged cell corresponds to the cell in the upper left corner of the original selection. If you merge several cells into a single cell, only the contents of the cell in the upper left corner are kept.

■ Adding shading to a table

You can add shading to decorate the background of a table, a paragraph or a text selection. How is it done?

1. Click anywhere in the table.
2. Select the cells that you want to enhance with a backdrop.
3. Open the **Format** menu.
4. Select the **Borders and Shading** option.
5. In the Borders and Shading dialog, click on the **Shading** tab.
6. Specify your shading colour. The shading can be coloured, transparent, dark trellis, light diagonal and so on.
7. Click on the drop-down arrow of the **Apply to** list.

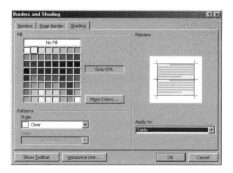

Figure 8.20 Add shading to your table.

8. Select the part of the document to which you wish to add shading.

9. Press the **OK** button to confirm your settings.

■ Adding a border to a table

You can add a border to one or more sides of a table. This border can comprise pictures, for example a range of trees or a stack of books. You can also embellish your table with a text box, an AutoShape, a drawing or imported ClipArt.

In Word 2000, by default tables are printed with a simple, unbroken, $\frac{1}{2}$ point black border.

To add a border:

1. Click anywhere in the table.

2. Open the **Format** menu.

3. Select the **Borders and Shading** option.

4. In the dialog, click on the **Borders** tab.

5. In the **Setting** and **Preview** areas, select the edge or edges that you wish to embellish with a border.

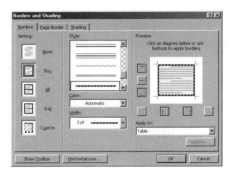

Figure 8.21 Specify a border for your table using the Borders and Shading dialog box.

6. Specify your border by setting style, colour and width.

7. Click the drop-down button of the **Apply to** list.

8. Select the part of the table to which you want to add a border (table, cell or paragraph).

9. Confirm your settings by pressing **OK**.

To get rid of the black ½ point table border displayed by default, perform steps 1 to 4, click on **None** in the **Setting** area and **Table** in the **Apply to** list; then confirm with **OK**.

■ Displaying or hiding the grid

If your table is set to have no borders – not even the default black ½ point table border – cells are shown separated by fine, dotted gridlines which help you to see which cell you are working in. These gridlines will not appear on the printed page.

To hide these gridlines, perform the following steps:

1. Open the **Table** menu.

2. Click on the **Hide Gridlines** option.

Conversely, if you want to display the grid, click on **Show Gridlines**.

Figure 8.22 The Display or Hide Gridlines icon.

■ Using AutoFormat

You use the **Table AutoFormat** command as follows:

1. Select the table.

2. Open the **Table** menu.

3. Click on the **Table AutoFormat** option.

4. From amongst the more than 40 table formats listed, select **Contemporary style**, for example.

Figure 8.23 The Contemporary style of the Table AutoFormat option.

■ Converting a table to text and vice versa

For whatever reason, a table can be converted into text. In this case, the columns are replaced by tabs, commas, paragraph markers or other separating characters. The reverse can be done provided that the intended columns are demarcated by unique characters.

1. Select the rows (or the whole table) that you wish to convert into text.

2. Open the **Table** menu.

3. Click on the **Convert Table to Text** option.

4. Select the separator character that you prefer.

■ Calculating the sum of a table row or column

To perform additions in your table:

1. Click in the cell where the total should appear.
2. Open the **Table** menu.
3. Select the **Formula** option.

   ■ If the cell you selected is at the bottom of a column of numbers, Word offers you the **= SUM (ABOVE) formula.**

   ■ If the selected cell is at the extreme right of a row of numbers, Word offers you the **= SUM (LEFT) formula.**

4. Click **OK** to confirm.

Figure 8.24 Performing calculations in Word 2000.

*Word offers a wide range of mathematical formulas. As standard the parameters used are either cell references of the type A2:C4, or bookmark references, or predefined values such as **ABOVE**, **LEFT**, **RIGHT**.*

■ Creating tables freehand

Being able to design a table freehand rather than copying and pasting an Excel table, or even going through the above steps, is a real advantage. In Word 2000, you can easily create columns and rows, arrange them and even modify them using the Draw Table (pencil icon) tool. Let's suppose that you want to create a table with four columns of five rows. Here is how to go about it:

1. Create a succession of plus and minus signs, for example +--------+------+---+------+.

2. Word 2000 interprets this sequence as a possible table structure and automatically converts it. The Assistant will ask you whether you wish to accept this conversion or change it back. You also have the possibility of turning this option off. Click on **Cancel** to keep the table and to leave the automatic conversion option switched on.

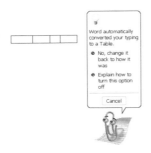

Figure 8.25 The Assistant tells you that Word has converted the + and - signs of your keyboard input into a table.

A table containing one row is displayed. The width of each column corresponds to the number of minus signs you typed in step 1. Let us assume you are creating a table of students' assessments in different subject matters.

3. Enter the column headings. The width of each column adapts to that of the heading (see Figure 8.26).

Figure 8.26 The headings row of your table.

4. Once the first row is finished, press the **Tab** key (on the left of the keyboard, above the **Caps Lock** key) to create a new row.

5. Enter the desired information into the new row. Once you have filled a row, new rows will be created, again by pressing the Tab key in the last column of a row.

Note that automatic width adjustment will only take place when a single word entered in one of the cells is longer than that column's heading. In case of several shorter words, the cell is instead spread over two or more lines (see Figure 8.27). To create a second line in a cell manually, simply press **Enter**.

Subject	Written	Oral	Assessment
French	12	14	Good
Maths	14	11	Good but could be better

Figure 8.27 Your table keeps growing.

6. Click anywhere in the table and adjust the column widths by using the mouse to move the column pegs on the ruler (see Figure 8.28).

Figure 8.28 The column pegs on the ruler can be used to change the width of each column.

Figure 8.29 Inserting columns with the Tables and Borders toolbar options.

7. To add a column to a table, either select the column to the left or right of which you wish to add the new column, or simply click into any of that column's cells.

8. Select the **View** menu, **Toolbars** submenu, then **Tables and Borders**. The Tables toolbar is displayed. Click on the arrow next to the bottom left button to open the menu of available options. Select **Insert Column to the Right** or **Insert column to the Left**.

Tables within tables

One of the more interesting innovations in Word 2000 is the possibility of splitting a table cell in such a way that it, in turn, can contain a table. Returning to the last example, let's suppose that you want to detail an item, and break it down. You need the last cell just added on the right to contain a table of three rows of five columns:

- Select the cell to split.

- Click on the **Split Cells** tool in the **Tables and Borders** toolbar.

- In the dialog box that appears, specify and confirm the number of rows and columns.

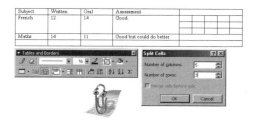

Figure 8.30 Splitting cells enables tables to be nested, in other words, to change the contents of a cell into a table.

Designing a complex table

To speed things up, you can use the **Draw Table** tool to design an even more complex table, like this:

- In the **Tables and Borders** toolbar, select the pencil icon.

- Keeping the left mouse button depressed, draw the rectangle which will hold the table.

- Draw the columns and rows one by one. As you begin, each horizontal or vertical line is prolonged as a dotted line. Release the mouse button.

- Draw a table within a table, following the same method.

- Use the Eraser tool to remove any errors.

Numerous variations are available, which enable sophisticated and original tables to be designed.

Subject	Written	Oral	Assessment					
French	12	14	Good.	Month 1	8	12	15	9
				Month 2	13	15	8	12
				Month 3	15	10	14	13
Maths	14	11	Good but could do better.					

Figure 8.31 Splitting cells enables the design of attractive and impressive tables.

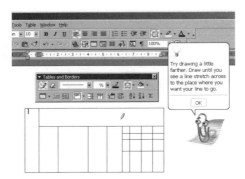

Figure 8.32 With the help of the Draw Table tool on the Tables and Borders toolbar, you can use your imagination to create complex freehand table designs. The Eraser lets you rectify mistakes.

9 Outline view

Structuring long documents

Creating a document outline

Assigning hierarchical levels to paragraphs

Displaying hierarchy levels in Outline view

Collapsing or expanding an outline

Promoting or demoting a level

Moving paragraphs up or down

Selecting text in Outline view

Numbering an outline

Printing an outline

Word 2000 Outline mode enables long documents to be structured. It assigns up to nine levels of formatted titles. The point of such a structure is to clarify your document design and layout.

■ Structuring long documents

Outline mode is designed for structuring long documents and to provide specific formatting.

Headings at each level are formatted with predefined heading styles (Heading 1 to Heading 9) and assigned to corresponding hierarchical levels (Level 1 to Level 9). You can automatically assign styles or levels to your headings. Word 2000 indents each heading according to its level. These indents are visible only in Outline view.

1. Open the tutorial text entitled **Expand the File** and click on the **New** option. In the dialog box click on the **Reports** tab, select the **Professional Report** button icon and click **OK**. The new report appears in **Normal View**.

Figure 9.1 A document in Normal view.

This document has a structure made up of different levels of text. Outline view will enable this structure to be seen and used. The first thing is to put the structure on display, then you can rearrange the headings and subheadings similar to the example used here.

2. Click on the **Outline View** button at the left end of the horizontal scroll bar at the bottom of the screen, immediately above the Status bar. Alternatively, you can expand the **View** menu and select the **Outline** option.

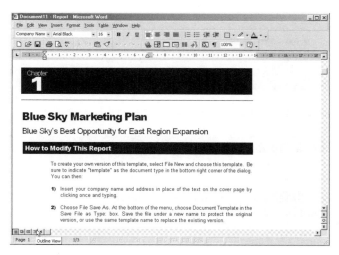

Figure 9.2 The Outline View button, at the bottom of the screen.

The new professional report appears in Outline view.

Notice that each component structure element is indented according to its hierarchical level.

 You can make an outline for an existing text or begin editing a text by organising headings.

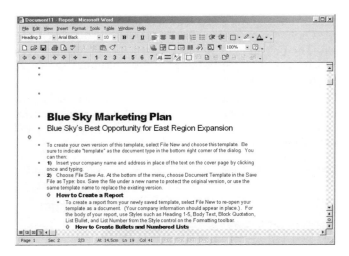

Figure 9.3 The document appears on the screen in Outline view.

■ Creating a document outline

There are three ways to make a document outline:

■ Organise a new document by entering the headings in **Outline** view. As you reorganise headings and subheadings, Word 2000 automatically assigns predefined heading styles to them. To manage your text more easily, reduce its screen length by displaying only the headings you need. It only remains for you to number them. To assign a level to a paragraph heading and apply the corresponding style to it, drag the symbols + and -.

■ Assign hierarchical levels to paragraphs to give your document a hierarchic structure. You can do this in **Normal** view.

- Create an Outline style numbered list. The text is not formatted with predefined heading styles. Outline numbered lists comprise of nine levels. To see them, open the **Format** menu, click on **Bullets and Numbering**, then on the **Outline numbered** tab.

You have chosen the second method, the assignment of hierarchical levels to paragraphs.

 Work in Outline view when you have to organise and structure the contents of a file.

■ Assigning hierarchical levels to paragraphs

To be able to process your document in Outline view, you have to give it a hierarchical structure. To do this, you have two choices:

- with predefined heading styles (Heading 1 to Heading 9);
- with hierarchical level paragraph formats (Level 1 to Level 9).

If you do not want to change the look of your document, use hierarchical levels applied by invisible formatting. Heading styles change the formatting.

Formatting paragraphs in Normal view

1. Work in **Normal** view.
2. Select the text to which you want to assign an Outline hierarchy level.
3. Open the **Format** menu.
4. Click on the **Paragraph** option.

Figure 9.4 The Outline levels of the Indents and Spacing tab
of the Format/Paragraph dialog box.

5. Click on the **Indents and Spacing** tab.

6. Click the **Outline level** drop-down arrow and set the desired level.

7. Repeat the operation as often as there are paragraphs of different Outline levels.

Your document comprises an Outline hierarchy structure of four heading levels.

■ Displaying hierarchy levels in Outline view

Having completed the preliminary work, go into Outline view. The structure of your document appears level by level.

The Outline view toolbar, with its buttons numbered from 1 to 7, lets you display the headings up to each level.

- Click on **1**: your level 1 heading is shown.
- Click on **2**: your headings at level 2 appear.
- Click on **3**: your headings at level 3 appear.

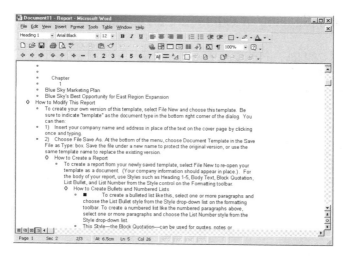

Figure 9.5 The clear layout of your document helps you to add any headings needed for easier processing.

- Click on **4**: your headings at level 4 are shown.

- Click on the **All** button: the whole of your document appears with its Outline levels.

- If you click on the **Show First Line Only** button (the one with the two parallel black lines icon, to the right of the All button), you see the structure of your document, as well as the first line of each paragraph.

- If you click on the **A/A** button next to it, you will see all the formatting in your document.

Figure 9.6 Displaying headings at level 1.

■ Collapsing or expanding an outline

- **Collapse an outline.** Show only headings of a level higher than the current level.

- **Expand an outline to a given level.** View all headings up to that level.

To collapse or expand an outline, use the numbered buttons on the **Outline** view toolbar.

The principle is: click on the number which matches the heading level number that you wish to display. To display all levels, click on the **All** button on the **Outline** view toolbar.

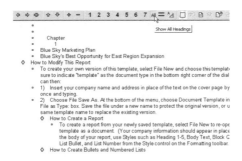

Figure 9.7 The whole of your document appears with Outline levels and headings that you added in Outline view.

- If you click on the **4** button and then on the **Collapse** button (the one with the – sign icon), you will get level 3.

    4 – 1 = 3

- If you click on the **2** button and then on the **Expand** button (the one with the + sign icon), you will get level 3.

    2 + 1 = 3

Figure 9.8 To collapse heading levels.

To collapse or expand heading levels, you can use the **Collapse** and **Expand** buttons on the **Outline** toolbar, or the + and − symbols of the outline itself.

■ Promoting or demoting a level

Raising or lowering a heading means to promote or demote it from its present Outline level.

To achieve this, you have two tools: the green right-arrow and left-arrow.

- The green left-arrow on the **Outline** toolbar promotes the selected paragraph to the next higher Outline level.

- The green right-arrow on the **Outline** toolbar demotes the selected paragraph to the next lower Outline level.

Hence, if you want to work on the structure of your document, to change the Outline level of a heading, use the green arrows pointing left or right.

In our example, the heading How to Create a Table of Contents has the same Outline level as How to Change a Header or Footer. If you think this is a mistake, that the heading ought to have the same Outline level as the heading More Template Tips, then:

1. Select **How to Change a Header or Footer**.

2. Click on the green arrow pointing to the left. Your heading is promoted to the same Outline level as **More Template Tips**.

This is a very useful procedure when you are working on a very long document. By working in Outline view, you manipulate the structure of a document at your ease by being able to view the Table of Contents and alter it at the same time as you alter the document itself!

■ Moving paragraphs up or down

Two green arrows, the one pointing down and the other up, assist you to move paragraphs.

- The green (**Move Up**) arrow pointing upwards moves a selected paragraph upwards, and also the collapsed (and currently hidden) text appended to it. It places the whole above the preceding displayed paragraph.

- The green (**Move Down**) arrow pointing downwards moves a selected paragraph downwards, and also the collapsed (and currently hidden) text appended to it. It places the whole below the following displayed paragraph.

■ Selecting text in Outline view

The method of selecting text, headings or paragraphs, in Outline view, differs from that in Normal view.

To select a heading, its subheadings and the body of the text:

1. Click on the white cross displayed close to the heading, or place the cursor to the left of the heading.
2. Double-click after the cursor changes into a white arrow pointing top-right.

To select only a heading, without its subheadings and paragraphs:

1. Place the cursor left of the heading.
2. Click when the cursor changes into a white arrow pointing top-right.

To select a paragraph of body text:

1. Click on the small blank white square next to the paragraph; or just place the cursor to the left of the paragraph.
2. Click when the cursor changes into a white arrow pointing top-right.

To select several headings or paragraphs:

1. Place the cursor to the left of the text.
2. When the cursor changes into a white arrow pointing top-right, drag the cursor up or down to select the desired text elements.

 *In **Outline** view, if you single-click to the left of a paragraph, the whole paragraph is selected.*

■ Numbering an outline

Having structured and formatted your text, you can number it.

To do this, execute the following tasks in sequence:

1. Open the **Format** menu.
2. Click on the **Bullets and Numbering** option.
3. Select the desired **Outline** level.

You can change to a personalised numbering by clicking on the **Customize** button.

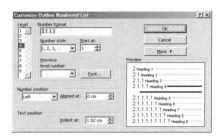

Figure 9.9 Your customised Outline numbered list.

Amongst the parameters you can use to customise a numbered Outline list are:

- Number format;
- Number style;
- Number position;
- Text position: indent;
- Number position: alignment;
- Style to link to level;
- Legal style numbering.

To number your outline, click on each heading level and confirm it.

Figure 9.10 The numbering applied to your outline.

■ Printing an outline

Once your document has been structured in different Outline levels, you can opt to print only the text outline or the text of specific Outline levels.

You are in Outline view.

1. Display, for example, the Outline level 1.

2. Click on **Print**.

Word 2000 prints only the Outline levels displayed. If the body of the text is visible, it will be printed in its entirety.

10

Doing a mailshot

■ Creating a data file

A mailshot, also called a *mailing*, consists of creating person-alised documents starting from a database and a form letter. Your form letter is a standard Word document.

A mailmerge consists in merging the form letter and the personal information stored in a database.

For example: you are the manager of a company. To correspond with clients, you are going to create a form letter and a file of clients in your database. The principle is equally applicable to a correspondence file, for a newsletter.

Choosing a form letter

The first step is to choose a letter template. Perform the following steps:

1. Open the **File** menu.
2. Select the **New** option.
3. Click on the **Letters and Faxes** tab.
4. Choose a letter template. Click on **OK**.

Figure 10.1 A professional letter template.

Opening Mail Merge

The second step is to use the **Mail Merge** utility.

1. Open the **Tools** menu.
2. Select **Mail Merge...**

A dialog box titled **Mail Merge Helper** appears on the screen.

Figure 10.2 The Mail Merge Helper dialog box.

3. Click the **Create** button.
4. Choose the **Form Letters** option.
5. Choose **Active Window**.
6. Press on the **Get Data** button.
7. Click on **Create Data Source...**

Word 2000 offers a list of commonly used field names. You can add or remove fields as you wish.

For a mailshot addressed to clients, the LastName, Address1, City and PostalCode fields will be fine.

Figure 10.3 Selecting the fields of your choice.

8. Confirm by clicking on **OK**.

9. Give your file a name – Clients.

10. Save this new file in the folder L10, for Chapter 10. A dialog box informs you that the data source you just created contains no data records, and offers you two choices. Choose **Edit Data Source** to access the database.

Figure 10.4 By clicking on Edit Data Source, you access the database to create the addresses.

11. In the fields, enter the details for the first client.
   - Smith
   - 100 East Street
   - Sheffield
   - S10 1DJ

Add this first record to your database, the Clients file, by clicking on **Add New**.

Continue adding records for the other five clients:

- Clark
- 32 Alton Street
- Peterborough
- PE1 3AB

- Dugdale
- 20 Rose Avenue
- Leeds
- LS1 7RL

- Reed
- 45 Queen Street
- Louth
- LN11 1AY

- Law
- 11 Highland Road
- St Andrews
- KYI6 4ES

- Dunham
- 7 Valley Road
- Sheffield
- S8 9TF

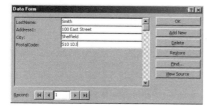

Figure 10.5 Entering the data.

You can remove or add records, modify them and search for them. When you have finished working, confirm your entries by clicking on OK.

The letter form then appears on the screen.

1. Place the insertion point in the place where the FirstName merge field should be.
2. Expand the **Insert Merge Field** button on the Mail Merge toolbar.

Figure 10.6: Using the Insert Merge Field on the Mail Merge toolbar.

3. Select the **FirstName** field that appears.
4. Click to confirm.

The word LastName appears in your Form Letter.

5. Repeat this operation for the three other fields: Address1, City and PostalCode.

Figure 10.7 Your letter template with the fields inserted.

■ Creating a form letter

Once these fields have been inserted, fill in the rest of the template:

- the company name:
  Cybertechnics
- its address:
  Banners Building, Attercliffe Road, Sheffield, S9 3QS
- the date:
  29 July 1999
- the subject:
  newsletter
- the text:
  Dear Sir,

  We are enclosing our latest newsletter for the month of July.

  As you can see, our company has been expanding, adding new hardware and new staff, to be able to offer our clients enhanced services.

  Our sales team will be happy to arrange a visit to your premises, to discuss your requirements, but you can also visit our Website (www.goldcom.co.uk).

  Looking forward to hearing from you,
- the signature:
  Mervyn Hudson, Marketing

■ Displaying the result of a merge

Click on the **Merge to New Document** button to display the merge result.

Word 2000 has merged your form letter with the Clients database file. Your letter and the inserted fields are instantly translated to another document called Form Letters1.

cyber|technics

Banners Building
Attercliffe Road
Sheffield
S9 3QS

29 July, 1999

Smith
100 East Street
Sheffield
S10 1D.

Dear Sir or Madam:

Figure 10.8 Form Letters1 showing the merged client details for Smith.

 *The **Check for Errors** button shows errors in either the main document or the data source. Correct errors, if any, before starting the merge.*

■ Printing a form letter

To print your form letter, starting with Form Letter1, simply click on the **Print** button. Just one letter will be printed, the one addressed to the client Smith.

■ Printing a mailshot

To print the whole mailshot addressed to all six clients:

1. Select your merge document.
2. Click on the **Merge to Printer** button.

This function performs the merge and prints the results.

Your six letters are printed!

■ Setting merge parameters

If you want to modify the mailshot printing, press the **Mail Merge** button to bring up the **Merge** dialog box.

Figure 10.9 The Merge dialog box in which you can set options for the current merge.

For example, you can specify:

■ A selection of records to be merged, for example, those from record three to record six. To do this, use the radio buttons and entry fields in the Records to be merged section.

■ A merge to fax. Open the menu in the **Merge** to section, then select **Fax**.

■ Filtering records

If you do not want to merge all the information in the data file, you can set conditions for the merge.

The Query options allow you to select data records from the data file. To access them, perform the following:

1. Click on the **Mail Merge** button, on the right of the **Mail Merge** toolbar.

2. Click on the **Query Options...** button.

You have the choice between two tabs: **Filter Records** and **Sort Records**. Filter Records allows you to select specific records.

Let's say that you do not want records with names going from A to D to be included:

3. Select the **Filter Records** tab.

4. Click on the first pull-down arrow in the **Field** area and select the **FirstName** field.

5. In the **Comparison** area, click on the **Greater than or equal** formula.

6. In the **Compare to** area, enter **D**.

To set additional selection conditions, click on **And** or **Or** to link your conditions to one another.

Figure 10.10 Defining your selection criteria.

■ Sorting records

To merge records in a specific order, click on the **Sort Records** tab, then on the fields offered for entering your sort criteria. For example, you might decide to merge the Clients file in descending alphabetical order.

1. Click the pull-down arrow in the **Sort by** text area and select the **FirstName** field.

2. Use the **Descending** radio button.

Figure 10.11 Select the FirstName field to sort your records
in alphabetical order.

■ Creating mailshot labels

Producing mailing labels for a mailshot is done in the same
way, although the specification of the label size is a supple-
mentary option.

1. Open the **Tools** menu.

2. Click on **Mail Merge**.

3. Open the **Create** menu.

4. Select the **Mailing Labels...** option.

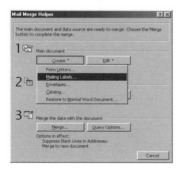

Figure 10.12 Creating mailshot labels.

In the Product number area, select a label type with the same dimensions as your labels. For example, 2160 Mini-Address.

Figure 10.13 Selecting a label type.

To find out more, click on the **Details...** button. You will have a preview of the presentation and form of the label. Size information is given for the following:

- the address;
- the top margin;
- the side margin;
- the label height;

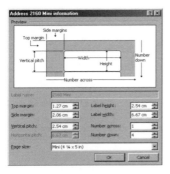

Figure 10.14 The selected label form.

- the label width;
- the page.

If the form and format of the label does not correspond to those of the label you have created, click on **Cancel**.

If the form and format of the label corresponds to those of the label you have created, use the selected label.

The label name
In the **Label Options** dialog box:

1. Verify the printer type.
2. Click on **New Label...**
3. Enter a name in the **Label name** input area.
4. Click the **OK** button.

The new label is listed in the **Product Number** area under the name My Label – Custom.

Figure 10.15 My Label is listed in the Product Number area.

 Measure the exact dimensions of your labels. The stated dimensions when purchased can vary slightly from the actual physical dimensions.

Any differences, which may be minimal, will reveal themselves during printing.

■ Printing labels merged with a list of addresses

The address book

You can print labels from your address book.

1. Open the **Tools** menu.

2. Select the **Mail Merge...** option.

3. In section 1, **Main document**, select **Create/Mailing Labels**.

4. When prompted for confirmation, click on the **Active Window** button. The active document becomes your main document for the merge.

5. In section 2, **Data Source**, select **Get Data/Use Address Book**.

6. In the **Use Address Book** dialog box, choose the address book you want to use and confirm by clicking on **OK**.

7. Word then asks you for confirmation to finish setting up your main document. Click on the **Set Up Main Document** button.

8. In the **Label Options** dialog, which pops up next, select the printer type and the type of label.

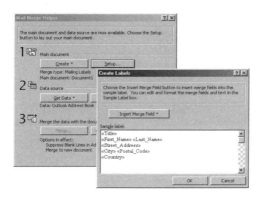

Figure 10.16 Inserting merge fields from your address book.

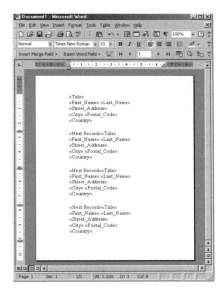

Figure 10.17 Merge fields formatted for label printing.

9. In the **Create Labels** dialog box, insert the fields to be merged from your address book

10. In the **Mail Merge Helper** dialog, click on **Merge**.

11. Click on **Printer** in the **Merge to** pull-down box.

Creating an address list

You have just printed some mailshot labels by merging names and addresses listed in an existing address book.

The procedure is slightly different if you want to create the list of addresses.

1. Open the **Tools** menu.

2. Select the **Mail Merge** option.

Figure 10.18 Compose your list of fields.

3. In section 1, **Main document**, click on **Create/Mailing Labels**.

4. Click on the **Active Window** button to make the active document become the merge main document.

5. In section 2, **Data Source**, click on **Get Data/Create Data Source**.

6. Define the records. Each data source constitutes a record.

The first line, called the Header row, comprises the names of the merge fields. Word 2000 offers a list of commonly used field names.

7. Remove or add the names of your choice.

11
Printing

■ Opening the Print dialog box

A printer installed under Windows is automatically available in Word 2000. Printing is therefore a very simple operation.

The first thing to do is select the **File** menu, then click on the **Print** option and examine the **Print** dialog box which opens before you.

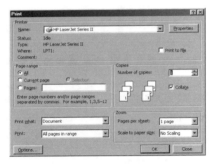

Figure 11.1 The Print dialog box.

A list of various options is displayed. The first, and most obvious, concerns the choice of printer. If you click the pull-down arrow to the right of the Name box, you will obtain a list of printers installed on your computer. If you only have one printer, it will already be selected. If the name of your printer does not appear in the offered list, it means that it's not installed.

■ The Control Panel

The system shows only installed printers. For example, imagine that you have bought a new colour printer for occasions when you have to output colour graphics or charts. You may use it only for 10% of print jobs, when you issue reports with charts in colour. Nevertheless, you must define your colour printer in your list of available printers. For that, open the Printers folder in the Control Panel and then install the appropriate driver with the aid of a floppy disk or a CD-ROM. Since then, your system will be aware that it has two printers. Under Windows, the existence of additional printers only points to the presence of the peripheral driver, which does not mean that the printer in question is switched on, or even that it is currently connected to the computer by cable. To switch from one printer to the other:

1. Click on the **Start** option of the Status bar.
2. Select the **Settings** submenu.
3. Choose **Control Panel**.

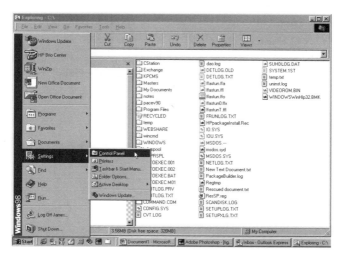

Figure 11.2 Accessing the Control Panel.

■ Installing a printer

The Control Panel appears on the screen.

Figure 11.3 The Printers option on the Control Panel.

4. Click on the **Printers** icon.

You have two choices:

- **Add Printer.**
- The printer is already installed on your system. In the case of our diagram, that would be the HP LaserJet Series II.

Figure 11.4 Select one of the two options.

The Add Printer Wizard

5. Select the **Add Printer** option. The **Add Printer Wizard** helps you to quickly install your printer.

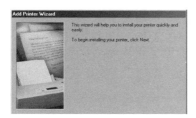

Figure 11.5 The Add Printer Wizard helps you to install your printer.

6. Click on the **Have disk** button if the new printer to be installed is delivered with an installation disk. A dialog box requests you to insert the diskette containing the printer driver. The default drive is **A:**.

7. Select the port you wish to use in the **Available Ports** list.

8. Click on **Next**.

9. If necessary, configure the printer port by clicking on the **Configure Port** button.

10. In the dialog box, enter a name for your printer (you can retain the name used by the manufacturer).

11. If you want this printer to be the default printer, select the **Yes** option. If not, choose **No**.

12. Click on **Finish**. Word asks you to insert an installation diskette.

13. Insert the installation diskette containing the new printer driver.

14. Click on **OK** to confirm.

15. Enter the access path for your new printer driver.

As soon as the installation is complete, Word 2000 displays the Printer dialog box again.

1. Open the **File** menu.
2. Select **Print**.

3. Click on the **Properties** command button.

4. In the dialog box for the selected printer, click on the **Paper** tab and set the desired options.

For example:

- Paper size;
- Upper tray;
- Orientation: **Landscape** (horizontal), **Portrait** (vertical).

Printer already installed

If you click on the icon for the printer already installed, namely HP Laserjet Series II, you can see information about the documents in course of printing, such as:

- Document name;
- Status;
- Owner;
- Progress;
- Started At.

Figure 11.6 Information on current print jobs.

■ Selecting the text to print

You have installed a printer that you like, and now you want to select documents to print:

1. Open the **File** menu.

2. Select **Print**. The **Print** dialog box is now displayed, set up for your printer following your use of the Control Panel.

3. Choose one of three options offered in the **Page Range** section.

   ■ **All.** The whole of your document will be printed.

   ■ **Current page.** Only the page containing the insertion point will be printed.

   ■ **Pages.** You have to specify the pages you want to be printed. If page 3, enter 3. If your document comprises seven pages and you want to print pages 4 to 6, you must enter 4-6 in the Pages box. Be sure not to omit the hyphen between the two numbers!

■ Specifying the number of copies

To set the number of copies:

1. Open the **File** menu.

2. Select **Print**.

3. Use the higher-lower arrows to set the number of copies in the **Number of copies** field to 2. Let's say also that your document comprises two pages:

   ■ If the Collate option is selected, Word 2000 first prints the whole document, page 1 and page 2, before going on to the duplicates and printing pages 1 and 2 again.

   ■ If the Collate option is not selected, Word 2000 first prints two copies of page 1, then two copies of page 2.

■ Printing odd and even pages

1. Open the **File** menu.

2. Select **Print**.

3. Use the pull-down arrow of the **Print** field and select one of the displayed options.

You can specify the pages to be printed:

- All pages in range;
- Even pages;
- Odd pages.

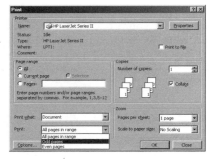

Figure 11.7 Selecting Print Odd pages.

■ Choosing print options

To choose print options:

1. Open the **File** menu.
2. Select **Print**.
3. Click on the **Options** button in the **Print** dialog box.
4. In the dialog box which opens, in the **Print** tab, tick the boxes for the desired options.

In the Print tab, you will find four groups of options:

- Printing options;
- Include with document;
- Options for current document only;
- Default tray.

Figure 11.8 The Print tab.

The Printing options are:

- **Draft output.** Word 2000 prints the document with minimal formatting and removes most graphics.

- **Update fields.** Updates all the fields in a document before printing it.

- **Update links.** Printing takes account of the latest changes to a linked object, for example a drawing (.bmp format) linked to a text file (.doc format).

- **Allow A4/Letter paper resizing.** For some countries, the standard paper size is letter, for others it is A4. Select this check box if you want Word to automatically adjust documents formatted for another country's standard paper size, so they print correctly on your country's standard paper size. This option affects the print-out only, not the formatting in your document.

- **Background printing.** You can continue working while your document is printing, provided that your computer has enough RAM memory and a hard disk fast enough not to slow down your other applications. Background printing uses more system memory. To speed up printing, deactivate this option box.

■ **Print PostScript over text.** You can send PostScript code to your printer by inserting PRINT fields in the text of the document. Word 2000 sends the printing commands as PostScript code. The PostScript commands embodied in your document are executed in the order of their insertion. This is rarely of interest to most users.

■ **Reverse print order.** Word 2000 prints the document starting with the last page.

■ Printing document properties

You can print a document's properties, as well as such items as comments, hidden text or drawing objects.

Printing the properties without printing the document

You can print a document's properties without printing the document itself:

1. Open the **File** menu.

2. Choose **Print**. The **Print** dialog box appears on the screen.

3. Click the pull-down arrow to expand the **Print what** menu and choose **Document properties**.

Printing the properties and the document

You can print your document as well as its properties, comments, markers, field codes, hidden text, drawings etc.

1. Open the **Tools** menu.

2. Click on **Options**.

3. Select the **Print** tab.

4. In the **Include with document** section, tick the boxes which match the specific items that you want to appear in your printed document.

  ■ Hidden text;

- Drawing objects;
- Comments;
- Field codes;
- Document properties.

 *You can print the automatic inserts. For this, open the **File** menu, click **Print**, then select **AutoText** entries in the **Print what** pull-down menu.*

■ Using two different paper feeds for a single document

Not all printers provide this function.

1. Open the **File** menu.
2. Select **Page Setup**.
3. Click on the **Paper Source** tab.

- To specify the paper feed tray necessary for the first page of your document, click on the desired feed listed in the **First page** scroll list.
- To specify the paper feed for the following pages, click on the desired feed in the **Other pages** scroll list.

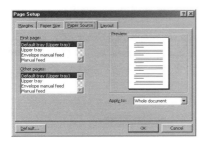

Figure 11.9 Selecting your two paper feeds for printing a single document.

When it's just part of a document and not more than one page, select **This section** in the **Apply to** menu before specifying the paper feed.

■ Selecting a paper feed tray

To select a paper feed tray:

1. Open the **File** menu.
2. Select **Print**.
3. Click the **Properties** button.

   The paper source can be:

   ■ top tray/paper input bin;
   ■ manual feed;
   ■ manual envelope feed.

■ Cancelling printing

To cancel printing, your have three options. You can:

■ click on **Cancel**;
■ press **Escape** if background printing is turned off; or,
■ double-click the printer button on the Status bar.

If you are printing a short document and background printing is turned on, it's likely that the printer icon will not be displayed on the Status bar long enough for you to click on it!

12
Surfing the Internet

■ The Internet

For businesses
Only a short time ago, businesses had to rent dedicated lines or go through a variety of messy modem setup procedures to send their data from one branch to another. They sent messages, and received accounts and business reports. Today, thanks to the Internet and data encryption – using a secret code to ensure confidentiality – the same exchange of data is achieved at local telephone call rates.

For creative people
For artists and writers, working on the Internet is the opportunity to contact friends, editors, magazines and journals, for less than the cost of a stamp. Writing, research and production are carried out via the Internet, e-mail and chat rooms.

For those who would like to know more about something
The Internet puts the whole planet's networked resources at the user's disposal. You can now have instant access to a wealth of information, and also act on that information. Interplay between creators and consumers of information is now possible.

■ Connecting to the Internet

To gain access to the Internet, you need a modem and an Internet account with an Internet service provider (ISP), or, more simply, you may be able to use the network at your place of work.

If you have all these things but still have trouble with Net access, it can be, quite simply, that the site that you want to reach is too busy. Be patient and try again later.

■ Selecting the Web toolbar

The **Web toolbar** allows you to browse quickly through documents containing hyperlinks. You can use it to open the Start page or Welcome page on the Net.

Using the Web toolbar, you can add documents found on the Internet to your Favorites folder. It 'remembers' the last 10 documents that you have accessed with this toolbar or with a hyperlink.

To select the Web toolbar:

1. Open the **View** menu.
2. Click on the **Toolbars** option.
3. Select **Web.**

Alternatively, you can select the Web toolbar via the Tools menu:

1. Open the **Tools** menu.
2. Select the **Customize** option.
3. In the **Customize** dialog, select the **Toolbars** tab.
4. Select **Web** in the scroll list.
5. Click on **Close.**

The Web Toolbar appears on the screen.

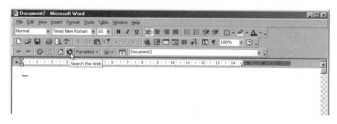

Figure 12.1 The Web toolbar.

The Word 2000 Web Toolbar lets you access your Web documents (html, htm, Jpeg, Gif and Gif animated formats) on the hard disk (off-line) as on a network once a connection is made.

■ Opening and changing the Start page

The Start page is the first to be displayed in the browser, when you launch it. Word calls the default browser, usually Microsoft Internet Explorer or Netscape Navigator. The Start page can be any Web site or a document on the hard disk of your computer. You can open this Start page from the Web toolbar. A Start page can contain hyperlinks to other computer documents.

To launch your default browser with your desired Start page, click on the **Start Page** button on the **Web** toolbar. If your screen does not show this toolbar, perform the following steps:

1. Open the **View** menu.
2. Click on the **Toolbars** option.
3. Click on **Web**.
4. Click on the **Start Page** button.

Changing the Web Start Page

1. Open the document you would like to use as a Start page.
2. Open on the **Go** menu on the **Web** toolbar.
3. Select **Set Start Page**.
4. Click on **Yes**.

When you change the Start Page with the help of the Web toolbar in an Office program, the new Start Page used in your Office programs is also used in your Web Explorer, provided it is Office compatible.

The Start Page icon launches the default Internet connection program, which you might have set to Internet Explorer or to Netscape, whichever you prefer. In this example and without prejudice, we have chosen Netscape. Against the background of Word 2000. the Internet screen appears as if for a normal session.

Figure 12.2 The Internet screen, set against the background of Word 2000.

To access the browser, click on its icon. First surprise: the Start page is not the one set according to the user's preferences, but Microsoft Network's home page, which means that Microsoft imposes its site by default.

In general the Start page is used to start exploring. It would be more logical to use the Alta Vista or Yahoo search engine! In certain cases, at the time of a first installation, MSN offers to download a complementary program (plug-in), such as Future Splash. Microsoft brings its contribution to the Internet by developing products intended to enhance the interface. If a

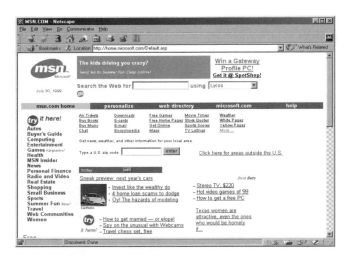

Figure 12.3 Microsoft's site loads by default.

Start page takes a long time to load, you have two available means of checking what is happening. The first consists of looking at the Status bar at the bottom of the screen. Details of current screen build-up are given in percentage terms. If loading times are excessive, deactivate the load images option. Things will then go seven or eight times quicker.

■ Searching the Web

To find Web sites on a particular topic:

1. Click on the **Search the Web** icon on the **Web** toolbar.

This tool gives usually gives access to the **Search Page of Microsoft**. Choose a search engine from the main ones.

2. In the text zone of the search engine, type a keyword that you want to search for. Imagine a man from Yorkshire who is on holiday in Australia trying to access his daily

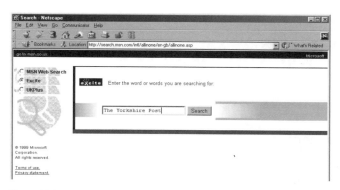

Figure 12.4 Using a search engine to find your site.

paper, The Yorkshire Post, for which he has forgotten the
Internet address.

After you have confirmed the search by clicking on the
Search button, the system gets under way.

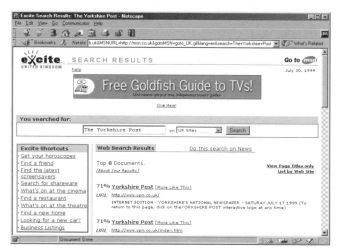

Figure 12.5 The search engine starts up.

Figure 12.6 The Web Page of the search target site appears on the screen.

After a time, the chosen search engine findings appear. What you see depends partly on how your monitor is set up. All you have to do is click on the ones of interest.

■ Opening Favorites

The **Favorites** icon is about favourite sites. This tool enables quick access to sites that you have bookmarked. When you open a document on the World Wide Web, or on a hard disk, add it to the Favorites folder. In this way, you can open it next time without having to remember its access path.

To perform this operation:

1. Open the **View** menu.
2. Select **Toolbars**.
3. Click on **Web**.

Figure 12.7 Select the Favorites icon on the Web toolbar.

4. The Web toolbar is displayed.

5. Open the **Favorites** menu on the Web toolbar.

6. Select the **Add to Favorites** submenu.

■ Go

This tool offers a shortcut to access previously visited addresses. It is also a chronological record of your visits.

There are four tools, at the extreme left of the toolbar:

- **Stop Current Jump.** Stop searching for a site. The search time for busy sites can be very long, and the user may tire of waiting and prefer to stop.

- **Refresh Current Page.** When a display goes wrong, with loss of data, you can correct the display by refreshing it.

■■

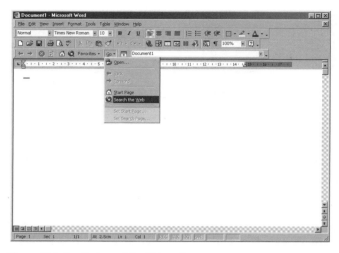

Figure 12.8 The Go icon of the Web toolbar.

- **Back.** To access the last file browsed.
- **Forward.** To access the next document in the history.

Last files used

The history contains the list of names of Web pages and files that you have already displayed while following hyperlinks in Office programs and on the Net. To open a recently saved file in Word, click below the opened File menu, on the first file name that appears.

You can program this list yourself and decide if it should be displayed or not.

Here's how:

1. Open the **Tools** menu.
2. Choose **Options**.
3. Click on the **General** tab.

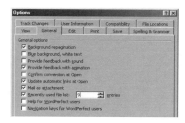

Figure 12.9 Displaying the last files used.

4. If you want to have the last files used listed below the opened File menu, activate the **Recently used file list** check box. You can have up to nine files listed.

5. If you do not want to have the history of your last visits displayed under the expanded File menu, deactivate the **Recently used file list** check box.

■ Adding an FTP site to your list of Internet sites

You can add an FTP (File Transfer Protocol) site to your list of Internet sites.

This is how to proceed:

1. Open the **File** menu.

2. Click on **Open**.

3. Click the **Look In** drop-down arrow, and then click **Add/Modify FTP Locations**.

4. In the **Name of FTP Site** area, in the **Add/Modify FTP Locations** dialog box, type the name of the FTP site you want.

5. If you wish to connect to an Anonymous FTP site (open to anyone), click on the **Anonymous** radio button in the **Log on as** area of the Add/Modify FTP Locations dialog box.

Figure 12.10 Adding an FTP location.

6. If you want to connect to an FTP site reserved for users with passwords, click on the **User** radio button in the Log on as area of the **Add/Modify FTP Locations** dialog box.

■ Creating hyperlinks

You can enhance your Web pages and Word publications by inserting hypertext links, also called hyperlinks. A hyperlink is a link that lets you jump from one location to another. A location can be a file on a hard disk, an Internet address, a bookmark or a multimedia file containing videos and sound.

The field of your hyperlink includes text underlined in colour. You have only to click on it to go immediately to the linked destination location.

You can insert hyperlinks yourself.

1. Open the **Insert** menu.
2. Click on the **Hyperlink** command. The **Insert Hyperlink** dialog box appears on the screen.

Figure 12.11 Inserting your Hyperlink.

3. Enter the path to the document you want to link to, or locate and enter the path to the document you want to link to using the **Browse** command.

4. If you want to jump to a specific location in the document, for example, a bookmark, a named range, a database object or a slide number, enter or locate that information in the **Named location in file** (optional) input box.

■ Stopping a search for a link

To cancel a prolonged search (some search times can be several minutes), you have to display the Web toolbar.

1. Open the **View** menu.
2. Select **Toolbars**.

3. Choose **Web**.

4. Click on the **Stop Current Jump** icon, once the Web tool-bar is displayed.

 *The **Stop Current Jump** button is available only when you open or activate a file on the Internet, on the World Wide Web, or on your business intranet (a local network), unless it is a file on your hard disk or on the office internal network.*

■ Saving documents on the Web

From Word 2000, you can create Internet sites, then save them on the Web. All you need to do is create a document and save it as a Web page. Thanks to the Web toolbar, Word 2000 enables the insertion of links and other objects, and the creation of more complex documents, suitable for the Internet and practically ready for use.

To save a document on the Web:

■ Open the **File** menu.

■ Select **Save As**.

■ In the file name box type the location for the FTP site, which is: **ftp://ftp.myworld.com.** Then click **Save**.

Figure 12.12 To fill in the FTP data, the server address must be known, as well as its ID and password.

Figure 12.13 An FTP site looks like a hard disk.

- In the dialog box which appears, fill in the input boxes relating to the FTP, and click **OK**.

- The FTP site is displayed exactly as if it was a part of Windows Explorer, that is to say, a completely separate hard disk. For small items, this facility avoids having to use dedicated software such as FrontPage.

Appendix
Installing
Office 2000

Installation on demand
Maintaining Office 2000

■■

As shown in Figure A.1, Office is installed using an **Installation Wizard**. Excel is only one of numerous component applications that make up the Office 2000 suite. The installation dialog box appears as soon as the CD-ROM is inserted into the drive. After the user has accepted the terms of the license contract, the software offers two types of installation:

- **Automatic.** Office 2000 installs all the standard components, without asking the user. This option is recommended for an easy and quick installation. On the other hand, there is no interaction and the user has no chance of choosing an installation folder, or a choice of different components. The components can, however, be customised afterwards.

- **Custom.** The user can choose both the installation folder for Office 2000 and for the component applications he wants to use. This option should definitely be chosen if you want to keep all or part of a previous version.

 You are strongly advised to defragment your hard disk before installing any large software application. This operation, which consists of regrouping widely spread data into consecutive

Figure A.1 Installing Office 2000.

> blocks on the hard disk, reduces read head movements on the
> hard disk and speeds up program execution. To perform this
> disk maintenance procedure, click on **Start**, point to **Programs**,
> **Accessories**, **System Tools** and select **Disk Defragmenter**. If
> you would like to know more about this command, consult your
> Windows 98 documentation.

If the Custom option was chosen – which is highly recommended – Office 2000 displays the dialog box shown in
Figure A.2; the upper text zone contains the path leading to
the folder where Office will be installed. If the default path
does not suit you, click on the Browse button; Windows
offers you the usual tree of folders in which you can navigate
to the one you want.

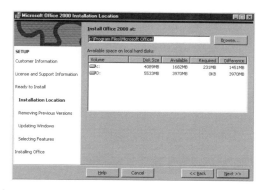

**Figure A.2 If you select the custom installation, you can choose the hard
disk and folder in which to install Office 2000.**

If the folder to hold Office 2000 does not exist yet, type its
name in the text input box, being careful to separate the
other folders in the path with a backslash (\). The Wizard will
create it automatically.

The window shows available hard disks, their size, available
space, space needed for a complete Office 2000 installation

and the space that will be left over after installation. Note that the disk occupation calculations only relate to the disk named in the text input box, the C: disk, in this case. If you want to install Office 2000 on the D: disk, for example, you have to show it in the text input box (the act of clicking in the window will have no result).

The dialog box shown in Figure A.3 is the most important in the procedure: it is here that you choose which components to install: Word, Excel, Access, PowerPoint, as well as various tools and files.

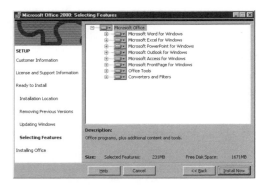

Figure A.3 In this dialog box you decide which Office 2000 components you want to install.

Click on the plus (+) sign of a component to expand a tree showing various elements. Each is preceded by an icon showing in what way it will be installed. It is important to examine each icon carefully, and perhaps to change some: click on the icon to change it and, as shown in Figure A.4, a menu in keeping with that icon will appear. It contains the options commented in Table A.1 (note that in some cases, only parts of these options are available).

Figure A.4 This contextual menu tells Office 2000 whether or not to transfer an element to the hard disk.

Table A.1 Installation options

Icon	Option	Comments
	Run from the hard disk	The selected component is transferred to the hard disk
	Run entirely from the hard disk	The selected component is transferred to the hard disk, including all the elements which depend on it, that is, those lower in the tree
	Run from the CD-ROM	The selected component can only be run if the Office 2000 CD-ROM is present in the drive
	Run entirely from the CD-ROM	The selected component as well as all the elements which depend on it can only be run if the Office 2000 CD-ROM is present in the drive
	Install only at the occasion of first use	These components will be installed on the hard disk only at the time they are first needed
	Not available	These components will not be installed

*Although the **Run** and **Run entirely** icons may differ in the context menu (the second is distinguished from the first by a colon), they are identical in the tree. This is why it's always recommended to open them up and check the components for installation.*

Carefully select all the components to be installed. If they are indispensable, install them on the hard disk. If you estimate that you will probably need them occasionally, set their icon to **Install only at the occasion of first use.** When you need one of them, Office will install the requested component.

If some elements should not have been installed (as can be the case with some rather intrusive Assistants), choose the **Not available** option. They will not be installed, unless you reinsert the original Office 2000 CD-ROM and choose the **Add/ Remove Components** option in the Maintenance dialog box.

The space that selected components will occupy and the remaining free space on the hard disk is displayed towards the bottom of the dialog box. Click on the **Install** button to transfer to the hard disk whatever must be transferred. A status indicator, or gauge, subsequently shows how the installation is progressing.

It's likely that a dialog box entitled **Remove Shared File?** (see Figure A.5) will appear during the installation. It signals that Office 2000 is preparing to replace an existing file with one of its own. It's often a file with a DLL extension (Dynamic Link Library) which means it might be shared by other applications. By default, the Office 2000 installer advises to keep the existing file, which is normal since it does not pose any problem. Click on **Yes** to keep it. Choose the **Yes To All** option for keeping everything, if this is offered.

When it has finished, the Office 2000 installer signals that it must restart the computer so that Windows can register the different program elements that have been installed. Click on **Yes.**

Figure A.5 Systematically opting to keep older versions of files.

■ Installation on demand

Installation on demand is a new feature of Office 2000; it has already been mentioned in Table A.1, concerning the **Install only at the occasion of first use** option.

The principle rests on a concept so simple that it is astonishing that nobody thought of it sooner. Up to now, the user had to choose the elements for installation on the hard disk. If, at the time of installation, certain files were judged to be superfluous – some modules, for example, of ClipArt – there was a strong risk of not thinking about them again later and even forgetting that they were ever on the CD-ROM. Other users transferred everything to the hard disk 'just in case...', thus wasting a lot of space.

With Installation on demand, the elements and files which are not installed are listed in the menus and dialog boxes of Office 2000 applications, although they do not exist on the hard disk, so they take up no valuable space. The first time you call for a function that has not been installed, the Office Assistant will display the message 'This function is not currently installed. Do you want to install it now?' If you want to install it, click on **Yes**. The Assistant will then ask you to insert the Office 2000 CD-ROM.

A function tagged as 'Not available' during the installation of Office will not be offered later. Only functions marked with the **Install only at the occasion of first use** *option will be offered.*

The Start menu

When a complete application has been marked with the **Install only at the occasion of first use** icon, it is also listed in the Start menu. It is only at the time when you want to use it that Office 2000 will ask you to insert the CD-ROM for its installation.

▪ Maintaining Office 2000

It is possible to add or remove Office 2000 components at any time; to do this, insert the original CD-ROM (if the CD does not start automatically, double-click on the file **Setup.exe,** in its root folder). A maintenance dialog box (see Figure A.6) then offers several options:

Figure A.6 Restarting Office 2000 from the CD–ROM displays the dialog box giving access to maintenance.

- **Repair.** If an application does not work because it lacks a file, or because it has been damaged, this option should be selected. Missing or defective files are then replaced by their equivalents, transferred from the original CD-ROM (which must be inserted in the drive). Two options are offered in the dialog box which appears after clicking on the **Repair** button:

  - the reinstallation of Office 2000;

  - the repair of errors which might have happened during installation.

  It is generally the second option that you will select. The operation leaves untouched any personal files you have created in the meantime and preserves preferences set for each application.

- **Add/Remove.** This button gives access to the dialog box when you select elements for installation immediately or at the time of first use. If some elements have been marked as Not available, it is possible to make them accessible again.

- **Remove.** This button completely uninstalls Microsoft Office 2000 from the hard disk. Personal files are, however, kept.

An installation is never final. At any time, the user can modify it, remove or add components, and configure Office 2000 to meet his current needs.

Index